Goin' Solo . . . at 20 and 30

The girl's guide to starting life on her own in a place she can't afford

WITHDRAWN KGL

Adina Kalish Neufeld

Creative
Minds
P
r
e
s
s

Reno, NV

Creative Minds Press
an imprint of **Beagle Bay Books**
Reno, Nevada
info@beaglebay.com

Cover Design: Melinda Macky

Visit our websites at:
www.goinsolo.net
www.creativemindspress.com
www.beaglebay.com

Library of Congress Control Number: 2004100855
ISBN: 0-9679591-1-X
First Edition
Printed in the United States
11 10 09 08 07 06 05 04   1 2 3 4 5

For Talia

Contents

Acknowledgments

You'd think a book about doing things on your own wouldn't have an acknowledgment section. On the contrary. Yes, most of the process (both the writing and the actual process of getting to the writing) was solitary, but I couldn't have done it without the support of so many individuals. First, to the hundreds of women who shared their own experiences *goin' solo*, including my friends and family, thank you. From networking to living alone, their stories and advice are much appreciated. A special thanks to all of the experts who agreed to share their infinite wisdom: Judith Beck, Ph.D., Director of the Beck Institute for Cognitive Therapy and Research and Clinical Associate Professor of Psychology in Psychiatry, University of Pennsylvania, Gene Blumberg, Certified Public Accountant, Bruce Felton, Writer, Judith Felton, CSW, Psychoanalyst, Scott Kays, CFP, President of Kays Financial Advisory Corporation, Karen McGee, Director of the Newhouse Career Development Center at Syracuse University, Eric Preston, Handyman extraordinaire, Karen Schaeffer, CFP, President of Schaeffer Financial, and Samantha Rifkin, Financial Analyst, Private Wealth Management, Goldman Sachs.

I want to express my sincere gratitude to Chris Tomasino for helping me get the concept of *Goin' Solo* off the ground and to Madelyn Larsen for knowing how to read a contract. A hearty thank you to my research assistants: Jillian Ferrigno, Allison Knab, and Holly Myers, all of them survival gurus in their own rights. And to my brothers, Michael and Alex, both of whom are a constant source of motivation, creativity and so many laughs.

Most importantly, I want to thank my husband, Kenny, who is my best friend. From reading numerous drafts at all hours to sharing in all of the highs and lows along the way, a girl couldn't ask for a better (or better-looking) guy. Of course, words cannot begin to describe my feelings for my daughter, Talia, who reminds me on a daily basis that there's so much more to life than work.

Lastly, I want to thank everyone who has ever said "No" to me before. You've given me more inspiration than you'll ever imagine.

Goin' Solo . . . at 20 and 30

Introduction

They say it's supposed to be the best time in your life
. . . your twenties into your thirties. But who are *they* anyway?
Youth is one thing, knowing what you're doing with your life
and where you're doing it is another. All of a sudden you're
supposed to be a responsible adult, balancing a career and your
finances, while at the same time trying to find your soul mate?
Not to mention having to answer everyone's annoying questions about your plans. And what if you don't want what's "right
for you" anyway? Debt, health insurance, moving, networking,
chasing your dreams—staying sane! It's more than a little overwhelming if you ask me.

Goin' Solo . . . at 20 and 30 is a book for women who are in
the process of figuring it all out. Maybe you're thinking of moving to a city but don't know if you can afford it. Maybe you've
toyed with the idea of opening a business but don't know where
to start. You may be single or dating, you may have a job or be
unemployed, but what you share with thousands of others right
now is that you're embarking on something on your *own*. You're
stretching outside of your comfort zone, perhaps for the first
time in your life. And wouldn't it be nice to have a little extra
help along the way?

Goin' Solo is meant to be used as a resource guide. Throw
it in your purse, read it on the train on your way to an interview
or when you're looking for an apartment. Take notes in the back
and add your own list of favorite *goin' solo* spots and deals. The
tips come from my own experiences *goin' solo*, as well as from
hundreds of women doing the same. Think of it as *tapas* for
your life. Some info here, a recommendation there, a money
saving suggestion, choice tidbits filled with websites and phone
numbers, but not too much where you don't need it. If you want
more information, you'll be directed where to go. You'll find the
resource sections heavy on cities like New York, Chicago, San
Francisco and Los Angeles, simply because they're some of the
most challenging places to live from a financial perspective. But
there's plenty of resources listed for other cities to give you a ba-

sis for comparison. And the advice, how-tos and life tips? They apply to everyone, no matter where you are. Hey, nobody said *goin' solo* is easy, but at one time or another, we've all been there. Might as well make the best of it, don't you think?

Chapter 1
Keeping House
Finding your first place; then actually living in it

I really had no business moving to New York City after graduating from college. With no job, no place to live and not one contact, I'm not exactly sure what I was thinking. But maybe the fact that I *wasn't* was how I survived. New York to me was a test, the ultimate challenge, where the rich people lived and where I was going to be like them. Yeah, I know, I've seen every other bright-eyed kid get off the bus thinking she's gonna be a star, but I wanted my shot, too. After pounding the pavement, assessing the competition, facing the rejection and even getting a couple of "yeses" along the way, eventually I realized that it wasn't about being a star at all; it was just about being there, on my own, without anyone telling me what to do or how to do it. This, in itself, was hard enough. With no family nearby, I never felt so petrified and liberated at the same time. Some days really sucked. And the good days were simply those that didn't suck. Sound familiar? I'm with ya.

Growing up hits you like a ton of bricks. One day you're running around without a care in the world. The next thing you know, your parents are moving to Florida and you're supposed to figure out what to do with your life. Yikes. While growing up means many things to many people, it's mostly about taking charge of *you*. There are lots of ways to do this, but one of the fastest ways to kick that process into gear is to move out on your own. Living at home to save money is sometimes a necessary means to an end, but sooner or later you're gonna have to leave your Snoopy sheets behind. Assuming you're physically able to care for yourself and you're ready to take that big step, this chapter's for you.

Bye-Bye Mom and Dad!

Looking for your first place can be a daunting experience. There's a lot to consider, especially if you're on a tight budget, or if you're not even sure where you want to live. For those who may be considering a move to a big city like New York, Los Angeles or Chicago, it can *really* be scary, especially if you

5

don't have a job. Maybe you'll need a roommate. Yeah, I know. Already did that in college. Well, there are ways to make this experience a little less "sorority-like," shall we say. You know, no more couches on the porch or communal showers. While it may not be the most enticing option, getting a roommate is a great way to save money. The tricks to keeping your lives separate will follow later.

Choosing Your City

If you're looking to move somewhere exciting but don't have a clue where to go, check out some of the cities listed at the end of the chapter. Here, you'll find some of the most expensive and difficult ones to conquer in addition to some other good choices for rent comparison, with info on how to get a deal without getting taken for a ride. The resources can help you get started and they're all free. You can also compare salaries in different cities as well as find lots of other useful moving information by logging on to www.homestore.com and clicking on the salary calculator. For more personal advice on different cities, log on to www.fodors.com and click on the "Talk" section. Here, you'll get candid recommendations from people around the globe on anything from travel tips to dining to traffic in a particular city, all on a very organized message board. Another fun site is www.findyourspot.com. You'll answer a host of questions about what you like and what you're looking for in a city. In turn you'll get an extensive listing of places tailored to you!

Finding That First Apartment

Since each city offers its own excitement and challenges, it's best to do your research ahead of time. If you were lucky enough to get a new job with an employer who's willing to pick up the tab on your move, your expenses and a real estate agent will be thrown into the deal. If you're moving to try someplace new just for the experience or you're embarking on your acting career, you won't get set up with *squat*. No matter where you decide to move, spend some time combing the town. You'll get the most information about apartments by walking around and into buildings, talking to doormen and the dog-walking neighbors. Take a notebook; hop on the public transportation. Drive around or pound the pavement. You'll be surprised at how much you can actually learn about the area this way.

So, Where Do I Begin?

• **Contact management companies** – Management companies generally operate large buildings, several in one city. By contacting the management company directly, you'll avoid the middlemen—the apartment brokers who charge a fee. Typically, this ranges from one to two months rent in cities like Boston, New York and San Francisco. Before you go to the brokers, try a Google search under "Apartment Management Companies" in your city and see what comes up. The often neglected phone book is another good resource. And every now and then while you're walking around, look up: management company names and phone numbers are sometimes listed on the buildings themselves.

• **Don't buy *no fee* rental lists** – In big cities, you often have to go through a real estate broker just to rent an apartment. The brokers make you (the tenant) pay a fee, ranging anywhere from 10 to 15 percent of the annual rent! You can avoid this by going directly to the management companies of the buildings (see the listings at the end of the chapter). There are some companies who'll try to capitalize on your naiveté by selling lists of what they claim are "No Fee Apartments." While a few places on the list may be legit, the majority of them will be outdated or completely incorrect. You'll lose your $300 and won't have anything to show for it. Whatever you do, don't buy these *no fee* lists.

• **Contact your college alumni association** – Alumni love helping alumni. It's just one of those things. Send an e-mail to your local alumni association asking if anyone knows of an available apartment in town and see what happens. You might get lucky.

• **Pray** – You don't really have to do this, but visit your local church or synagogue and post a sign on the bulletin board. Your mother will feel better about it too.

• **Look on Craigslist.org** – This is one of my all time favorite websites. It lists no fee apartments, many by owners themselves, in major cities all over the country. It has a great job board too. See for yourself at www.craigslist.org. Another good site is www.relocationcentral.com.

• **Consider house-sitting or working as a nanny** – This is a great way to score a place to live, especially for a short time while you're getting stared in a new city. Start by looking through bulletins from your local community center. Or, ask around if anyone needs a pet or plant sitter while they're on vacation.

Bottom Line: When it comes down to getting a good deal on an apartment, networking tactics (see Chapter Four: *Opening the Door*) apply. It's *always* about being in the know. And the more people you know, the better chance you'll have to get a place.

Before You Sign the Lease

Before you sign on the dotted line, make sure you do a thorough walk-through of the apartment. It's easy to get carried away, especially when the managing agent is standing over you telling you how lucky you are because there are five other people waiting outside who want this place. Look around and take note of everything. Ask as many questions as you can beforehand. Use the following list as a guide:

• **Appliances** – Are they clean and in working order? Don't be afraid to ask if anything can be replaced. Did you notice a nasty fridge door, a greasy stove top, a rusty sink? Things like this should be handled *before* you move in.

• **Lights** – Do they all work?

• **Counter Space** – Is there any?

• **Faucets** – This is one that most people overlook. Turn on all the faucets (don't forget the shower). How's the water pressure? You'll be showering here every day (hopefully) so make sure it's decent. Give the toilet a good flush too. Do this with the shower running and see what happens. Your roommate will thank you, especially when there's suddenly a frigid stream that's about to hit her. You'll probably find a lot of apartments that can't handle both at the same time but at least you can warn her in advance by yelling "Iceberg, dead ahead!"

• **Closets** – How many are there? Will the management company let you build another? Is there enough room for an IKEA armoire?

• **Windows** – Do they open and close well? If you're on a bottom floor, are there secure bars? In some states this is a requirement.

• **Locks** – How many locks are on the door? Make sure there are at least two, one of which should be a dead bolt. And ask about getting them changed as well. Who knows where those keys have been?

• **Electrical Outlets and Phone Jacks** – Are there enough?

- **High Speed Internet Access** – Is the building wired or is there wi-fi available? This is especially important if you'll be working from home.
- **Laundry** – Where's the closest laundry room? Is it well-lit and safe?
- **Floors** – Do they need resurfacing or sanding? Does the carpet need cleaning? Who pays for this?
- **Walls** – Will they be freshly painted?
- **Bathroom** – Is it clean? Same goes for the kitchen. Find out if the building will pay for a thorough cleaning job before you move in.
- **Storage** – Is there any additional storage in the building? What about a bike room?
- **Fire Escape, Sprinkler and Smoke Detector** – Older buildings have fire escapes. Newer ones have sprinklers and smoke detectors. These are musts. Make sure you ask if a fire escape route is posted in your apartment or in the hallway. Familiarize yourself with it.
- **Superintendent** – How accessible is the building Super or maintenance staff?
- **What's it like at night?** – If time permits, go back to the apartment at night. Check out the block, the lighting and the pedestrian traffic. It's important that you feel comfortable at all times.

Now, once you've found something you like and it fits your budget, be prepared to move on it. The more competitive the market, the faster you have to act. If you're planning to move to New York City or San Francisco, plan on looking for an apartment no more than one month in advance. And, make sure you show up with all the right documents in hand. These include a *current letter of employment, pay stub, bank statement, picture ID, tax returns* (if you're self employed) and *liquid assets* (things that can be liquidated or sold easily—read: cash). Liquid assets will be used to pay your first month's rent and security deposit (as well as your broker's fee if you got suckered into paying one). If you don't have any liquid funds (or, in cities like New York, if you don't make a certain amount to prove you can cover your annual rent), you're going to need a *local guarantor* or *co-signer* to help you out. A guarantor is just that—someone who will guarantee that your rent will be paid each month. Being prepared makes the difference between getting a place and not getting one. Most landlords won't even begin to process an application until all of the financials (everything listed above) are presented. So, if you're moving to a highly competitive real estate town, make sure you bring these documents to every appointment you make.

And one last thing, don't dress like a slob when you go to see an apartment. It makes a bad impression and you may lose a place because you don't look as serious as the next gal.

Legal Jargon

Apartment leases can be tricky, so make sure you read yours over very carefully. If you have a legal friend, fax it over to her for a quick look. Again, the more competitive the market, the more the landlords will try to get away with. In many cities you won't have much, if any, room to maneuver or revise the lease, but making yourself aware of your lease's restrictions will save you time and anxiety later. For example, make sure you find out the penalty for breaking your lease if you have to move out early. Will you simply lose your security deposit (generally one month's rent) or will you be forced to continue to pay rent until your lease is up? Are you allowed to sublet? How much will the rent go up after a year? What about pets? These little snags can mess up your entire living experience if you don't know the answers beforehand. For more information, pick up a copy of *Renter's Rights: The Basics* by attorneys Janet Portman and Marcia Stewart, Nolo Press. It's one the best no-nonsense guides to help renters like you. You can also log on to www.rentlaw.com and choose your state from the drop down list for specific information on landlord-tenant laws. In New York City, another good resource for tenants is www.tenant.net. In California, download the online guide: "California Tenants - A Guide to Residential Tenants' and Landlords' Rights and Responsibilities" from www.dca.ca.gov/legal/landlordbook.

Buying vs. Renting (a few quick words)

With interest rates at an all time low, the average age of a first time buyer has dropped considerably. So if you live in a city that's relatively affordable, do a mortgage calculation on www.bankrate.com to see if you're better off buying than renting. With tax deductions offered as incentives for first time buyers, you'd be surprised at how little a difference there is between a mortgage and a rent.

Now, if you live in New York City, for instance, that's

a whole different ballgame. In order to buy an apartment in Manhattan, no matter how great your credit is, you're going to have to put down at least 20 percent for your down payment, which is next to impossible for someone making $35,000. Even if you can do that, most apartments in the city are co-ops (short for cooperatives), meaning they're owned by the tenants themselves. Anyone who wants to buy in has to endure a co-op board interview. This process has been compared to being dragged through a car wash hair first and still coming out dirty. The point is, you can spend your entire year putting together an amazing package (consisting of *bank statements*, *tax returns*, *employer information*, *credit check*, lists of everything you own, extensive *letters of recommendation*, plus more), spend who knows how much making copies at Kinko's and impress the heck out of the board president, but if you owe even a nickel to your local grocer, you won't pass and you won't be able to buy in. Do I sound bitter?

So, a personal word of advice: unless you're rich, unless you're lucky and can find a condominium (which has different bylaws than a co-op) that doesn't require you to sign your life away (or you don't care that you'll have to sign your life away), then beware! If you plan on staying in New York City for at least five or more years and have the means, go for it! Just think about the process beforehand so you don't wind up in over your head. But remember, as hard as it is to buy a place in NYC, it's going to be just as hard to sell.

Mortgages

No matter where you live, you'll need to do research to get the best deal on a loan. Generally, you'll either take a fifteen- or a thirty-year mortgage. The main difference is that with a fifteen-year mortgage you'll pay a higher monthly payment but less interest. A thirty-year mortgage will allow you to spread your payments out over a longer period of time, but you'll wind up paying more in interest. A great place to start your mortgage research is by logging on to www.lendingtree.com. You'll have more banks compete for your business than you'll know what to do with. If you don't have the time to do your own research, I suggest going through a mortgage broker. You'll pay for the service, but you'll get a better deal without doing any of the leg work. Make sure you have the following on hand when you interview lenders: *employment information, Social Security card, info on income and debts, current address, type of property you're looking to buy, purchase price, down payment information, liquid assets and homeowner's insurance.*

Once You're In

Whether you're renting or a first-time home owner, congrats! You got a place! Nice work. Remember, you'll spend the most during your first few weeks. You'll need to have money for moving expenses, security deposit, phone and cable hook-ups, cleaning supplies and your first trip to the grocery store. Prepare to shell out at least $300 (more for a house) a week for the first month. It just happens that way. Also, don't forget to fill out a change of address form so everyone knows where to find you.

For those living in high-rise buildings, you'll also need to spend a bit extra tipping your doorman and building superintendent—somewhere around $20 to both—as soon as you move in. As annoying as it is, do this *immediately* to ensure you'll get good service throughout your stay in their building. If you don't have the cash to do this, give 'em $10 each and bake some cookies.

Construction

If you're lucky enough to get your own place, you rule! If you're stuck living with a roommate but can only afford a one-bedroom apartment, you're going to need a little privacy. One of the best ways to cut the cost of your $2200 one bedroom apartment in half is to literally cut your apartment in half. You can do this by hiring a handyman (or handywoman) to build a pressure wall in the living room. It's a good idea to check with your landlord before you do this. A pressure wall is designed to leave the existing walls in tact. It can be taken up and down so you don't scar the apartment. Sometimes you can get lucky and find an apartment that already has one up. In New York City, look for apartments in Murray Hill or on the Upper West Side (in the 90s). For some reason there are a lot of these there. Otherwise, expect to spend around $1500 to have someone put up a pressure wall in your place. Ask your handyman to make a window in the wall to allow for better air circulation. You can even hang curtains to make it feel like a real room. Make sure you use a licensed contractor in case of damage. Craigslist is a good place to start your search.

Décor and Other Projects

Roommate or not, it's important to make any space feel

like home. You can do this without spending a lot of money and still feel like you've left dorm life behind. The following is a list of unique little tips and projects that don't require a Ph.D. (aka: Phat Decorator) and just might do the trick, especially if you're in a small space:

• **Buy peel and stick tiles** – These sell for approximately $.50 a square and are easy to put over your cheesy linoleum floor. Buy them at any hardware store or Home Depot and they'll spruce up your kitchen. Try the black and white ones in the classic chessboard pattern for a retro, yet trendy look. They also make peel and stick carpet squares in all kinds of funky colors which look great in the living or bedroom. You'll find all kinds of modular flooring at www.interfaceflor.com. You can take them up with mineral spirits when you're tired of them—but prepare to spend some time doing it. Check with the landlord to make sure it's okay first.

• **Invest in multi-purpose furniture** – Don't just get a coffee table; get a coffee table that can actually store stuff inside (or use a trunk). In fact, do this for everything you buy. Try to find furniture with doors. It'll keep your apartment from looking cluttered and dusty.

• **Buy fold down tables** – For small spaces, these can't be beat. Crate and Barrel, Homegoods, K-Mart, Wal-Mart, Target (my personal favorite), Marshalls, T.J. Maxx, Straight from the Crate (NYC) and World Market all carry these small foldouts with little stools that can be stored underneath. Hide it in the corner when you're done eating.

• **Raid your grandmother's attic** – Antique trunks, old lamps, vintage linens—these items are priceless and are probably collecting dust somewhere in Florida. Ask your grandmother (or any other relative over the age of sixty) if she has anything to donate to your new digs. You'll come away with some truly unique items.

• **Slip into slipcovers** – Remember that ratty couch you stole off the porch of the Pi Beta Phi house? Get it steam cleaned. Do this before doing anything else. Then, invest in a slipcover (try www.surefit.com for some unusual patterns). You'll save yourself a few hundred bucks and won't have to think about how many people actually slept on that thing . . . at once.

• **Check out space-saver appliances** – Small kitchen? Keep your counters clear by getting space-saver appliances that can be mounted under wall cabinets. Look on eBay or www.overstock.com for this kind of stuff.

- **Use under the bed boxes and bags** – Store your seasonal clothing under the bed and you'll open up a whole new world of closet space. If your bed is on the floor, consider getting "Bed Lifters" (Bed Bath and Beyond or Linens and Things carry these) to raise your box spring off the floor to create more space.

- **Browse the flea markets and thrift stores** – Here you'll find anything from furniture to socks that can save you money when setting up your place. You'll have the best selection of stuff in the early morning, but you'll also have better bargaining power if you wait until the end of the day. Check out the city recommendations at the end of the chapter for some great finds.

- **Succumb to *Do-it-Yourself* furniture** – One word: IKEA. While not every city has one of these "disposable furniture" stores, if yours does, get there (www.ikea.com). The stuff is dirt cheap, durable and actually pretty cute. A couple of IKEA pieces mixed with your other furniture will keep your apartment from looking like a college dorm. They've got great space-saver solutions too. In New York, IKEA even offers free bus service to the New Jersey store. Also try Target (www.target.com), Wal-Mart (www.walmart.com) or Home Depot (www.homedepot.com) for other do-it-yourself furniture. You'll probably spend the afternoon shouting four letter expletives into the 2x4s and wonder why there are a million extra screws in the package, but you'll feel good when you're done assembling it. Crank up the tunes while you're doing this and in no event should you answer a phone call from your mother at the same time.

- **Don't mix business and pleasure** – If you're going to be working from home make sure you have an office "area," no matter how small, in a separate part of the room. A desk, a file cabinet and a place for your computer is good for starters. Keep this space clean and organized. Build shelves. Always think vertically. A jelly cabinet can hold files, papers, envelopes and all sorts of supplies. A decorative screen will do wonders for keeping your sleeping area separated from your pile of papers. Again, try to get furniture with doors so that when your workday is over, you won't have to stare at files when you're sitting on your bed.

- **Paint a wall red—or any other color** – Do this on

only one wall to add some spunk to the room. Try Barn Red, Butter Yellow or Periwinkle Blue (good for the bathroom). You'll need approximately one pint for every 400 square feet of wall space. Don't forget the primer. Then buy some stencils and give yourself a border on top. Check with the landlord before you do this. When you move out, you may have to paint over in white, but if it looks good the next tenant may want to keep it that way.

Necessities and Tools

Any woman living alone needs to be prepared. For what, you may ask? Anything from bugs to boys. Here's a list of some staples to keep on hand, passed on by gals *goin' solo* nationwide:

• **Keep A Full Tool Box** – Stocked with scissors, Philip's head and regular screw driver, hammer, pliers, wrench, tape measure, nails, picture hooks, glue and duct tape.

• **Don't forget the Bug Spray** – Little critters love big cities. Roach motels come in handy too. A broom is also good for getting those creepy-crawlers off the ceiling.

• **Buy mousetraps *a la* Tom and Jerry** – Not the glue kinds. These are the true *bona fide* mousetraps used with a piece of Swiss cheese. If you think you have a mouse, tape a plastic bag onto the floor and put the trap in the middle of the bag, so when the mouse is caught, you can just pick up the bag and don't have to touch anything. Then, feel free to scream at the top of your lungs.

• **Load up on condoms, tampons and Advil** – No roommate? Who you gonna borrow from when you run out? Keep a warehouse supply on hand.

• **Get Caller ID** – Anyone living alone should get this. It's easy and you'll avoid unwanted pests.

• **Block your caller ID** – Just because you see theirs doesn't mean they have to see yours. Protect your number from showing up on other people's caller ID by getting a block (the phone company can do this for you). Also, list your name in the phone book with initials only and no address.

• **Get Renter's Insurance** – Seems unnecessary but this could really come in handy if you ever have a problem in your apartment. For a nominal yearly fee, you're fully protected. For a quote in your area, log on to www.apartments.com and click on the moving center. Put in your zip code and you'll get a list of insurance agents in your area where you can compare quotes.

Make sure to ask your agent about *Loss of Use*, in case your apartment is damaged by fire.

Roommates

If you had to slice your apartment in half and put up a pressure wall, chances are you're living with a roommate. Roommates aren't always the easiest people to deal with, but they can help you save money, especially when you're starting out. If you do decide to buddy-up, keep some of these tips in mind. They'll make your life a little easier while you're sharing space.

• **Get two phone lines** – This is a must. I can't tell you how many arguments you'll avoid about missed messages or whose voice should go on the answering machine, not to mention the problems that arise when your roommate moves out without paying her last phone bill and *you* get stuck with the choice of paying it or wrecking your own credit rating. The investment will save you hundreds in legal fees (after you've beaten each other up). If you can't afford to do this and don't want to use your cell, then I highly suggest getting a voice mail service. For about $10 a month, you get a local number and a private outgoing message. Look under *Voice Mail* services in the phone book or ask your local phone provider if they have a service. It's worth it. If you're going to bypass the land line altogether, you might as well get the best deal on a cell phone. For the latest comparison of cell phones and plans, log on to www.getconnected.com.

• **Make schedules** – No, you don't need a chore wheel like in summer camp, but do have an idea who's going to clean and when. Do you both need to be out of the apartment by 7:30 a.m.? If so, consider showering in the evening or going to the gym before work. Little things like this can shave the annoyance off your day when you're waiting by the bathroom door wondering what the *heck* she's doing in there.

• **Decide what you're going to do about food immediately** – I hate those people who eat my cereal and then never replace it. Don't let that happen. When you move in, decide right away if you'll be sharing food. If not, pick your cabinets and start stocking up. Farmers markets are overflowing with cheap produce. You may even consider joining a food co-op. These wholesome alternatives to big grocery stores often provide fresh produce and food staples at low costs. You'll find a list of city co-ops at the end of the chapter.

If you decide to share food, lay out the ground rules together as a team. The first shopping trip will be your biggest. Load up on pasta, rice, canned goods, frozen dinners, soups, condiments, etc. Then, split the bill. Afterwards, you may want to set aside one day for shopping. If you can go together, great. If not, make sure you both agree to replace perishables when they're finished. Nobody wants to come home to an empty carton of milk in the refrigerator.

Another way to do this is to make a petty cash box. Every week, add $20 to the box and agree to use this cash for necessities only. You'll learn to be more frugal in the grocery store if you have a predetermined limit. If you have a list on the fridge of what's needed, you can take turns going to the grocery and make sure you stay stocked with the foods you both like. The bottom line when it comes to sharing food is consideration. If it gets to the point where you're the only one pitching in, it's time to have a little talk with your roommate.

• **Don't share furniture** – Food is one thing, furniture is another. Why? Because when you move out, you'll fight over how much you owe for the couch. Then you'll spend an inordinate amount of time explaining how it's devalued over time. Buy a few pieces for yourself and keep them when you leave. You'll save yourself money in the long run.

• **Know your bounds** – Is your roommate uncomfortable with you bringing your dates home? Maybe this is okay twice a month, but every Thursday, Friday *and* Saturday? Uh-uh. Decide before you move in what your "sleepover" rules are so you can both feel at ease. I've heard so many stories about roommates whose boyfriends conveniently moved in without paying rent. And then there were three. The guys weren't *officially* living there, but they might as well have been. So, even if you think you're cool with this, you may not be after a month of finding his boxers on your bathroom floor—especially if you're in a small apartment. Make it clear to your roommate before you move in that boyfriends or girlfriends need their own primary residence. You can even ask for proof of address. Just kidding. The point is this: Try not to turn the place into a frat house. You'll appreciate it when the tables are turned.

• **Know when to call it quits** – Having trouble with a roommate who was once your best friend? They say you learn the most about someone once you live with her. If you've given your living situation a fair shot and it's just not working out, maybe it's time to say goodbye before the friendship goes South.

Talk to your roommate about alternate living arrangements, such as moving to a larger place with more roommates or splitting up for good. Try not to screw your roommate by finding another place and leaving her to fill your spot. That's just not neighborly. List things on paper that are bothering you, such as leaving a messy sink, not cleaning the dishes or hogging the computer. Give her a month or two to see if she's responsive to your gripes. If not, it may be time to move on.

• **Be Flexible** – It's not a lifetime arrangement so recognize that everything won't always be done your way. Try and make the most of your living quarters so that you can actually call your place *home*.

City Specific Resources

Atlanta

Overview: A very affordable city with lots of action. Great singles scene too. You'll have no problem finding a place to live.

Average cost for a 700 square foot apartment: $800-$850.

Areas to check out: Decatur, Brookhaven, Virginia Highlands, Little Five Points, Vinings, Dunwoody, Buckhead (more expensive), and some new areas include Fairlie-Poplar and Castleberry Hill (www.castleberryhill.org).

Free Resources:

Free Apartment Locators
www.freeapartmentlocators.com
866.237.1401

Homestore
www.homestore.com

Creative Loafing
www.creativeloafing.com

Boston

Overview: This city isn't cheap. Generally, you'll find apartment brokers who charge an average of one month's fee just to rent a place. Try to avoid this if possible.

Average cost for a 700 square foot apartment: $1600

Areas to check out: Back Bay, Southend, Beacon Hill, North End, Charlestown. Try South Boston for slightly lower rents.

Free resources:

Boston Apartment Listings for sample listings (some with fees, some without).
www.bostonapartment.net
617.267.2340

Star Realty Group
617.731.0955

Alpha Management
www.bostonapartments.com/alpha.htm
617.789.4445

Resource Capital Group
www.resourcecapitalgroup.com
617.625.8315

Roommate Service:

Roommate Connection
www.roommateconnection.com
800-APT-SHARE

Chicago

Overview: Chicago offers a wide variety of apartments and lofts in lots of great areas. Compared to New York City rents, Chicago's a bargain!

Average price for a 700 square foot apartment: $850+

Areas to check out: Roscoe Village, Andersonville, Ravenswood, Lincoln Square, Bucktown (more expensive), Logan Square (West of Bucktown) Wicker Park, Pilsen, Rogers Park, Ukrainian Village.

Free Resources:

The Apartment Connection
www.theaptconnection.com
773.525.3888

The Chicago Reader
www.chireader.com

The Apartment People
www.apartmentpeople.com
3121 North Broadway
773.248.8800

Chicago Apartment Finders
www.chicagoapartmentfinders.com
906 West Belmont
773.883.8800

ICM Properties
www.icmproperties.com
773.549.5443

Kass Management
www.kassmanagement.com
2000 North Racine, Suite 3400
773.975.7234

Second City Rentals
www.secondcityrentals.com
1105 West Chicago Avenue, Suite 303
312.850.1316

Los Angeles

Overview: Sprawling, yes, but that also means more living

choices for you. The closer you get to the hills, the more expensive the rents. Plan to spend a lot of time in your car. But when you're driving around, don't forget to look up—lots of management companies list their numbers on the buildings themselves, especially in areas like Brentwood and Santa Monica. Something else to know about Los Angeles, many apartments don't come with refrigerators (go figure!). Make sure you ask if yours does.

Average price for a 700 square foot apartment: $1250

Areas to check out: Brentwood, Santa Monica, Manhattan Beach. Less expensive areas include: Silver Lake, Long Beach, West Los Angeles, Palms / Culver City, Mid-Wilshire (has lots of apartment buildings), Koreatown, Echo Park, Mount Washington, Highland Park, South Pasadena.

Free resources:

The Home Store
www.homestore.com (click on apartments).

Los Angeles Times
Online listings updated daily; routed through www.apartments.com

LA Weekly
www.laweekly.com/classifieds
Print edition comes out on Wednesdays. Online edition updated daily.

The Recycler
www.recycler.com
Print edition comes out on Thursdays. Online edition updated continuously. A very resourceful publication that is under utilized!

"The Original" Apartment Magazine
www.aptmag.com

Roommate Services:

Roommate Matchers
www.roommatematchers.com

Roommate Access (a national service)
www.roommateaccess.com

Miami

Overview: You shouldn't have too much of a problem scoring an apartment here either. You'll get a cheaper place if it's not *right* on the beach, but hey, can't have everything, right?

Average price for a 700 square foot apartment: $850 (more expensive in South Beach).

Areas to check out: Kendall, North Miami Beach

Free resources:

Rent Miami

www.rentmiami.com

New York

Overview: This one takes the cake for being the most expensive and most difficult city to score a place to live. You have to really use your noodle, as there are very few free resources in NYC. A handful of management companies who don't charge a fee are listed below. The list excludes luxury buildings, which are too expensive for me to recommend in good faith.

Average price for a 700 square foot apartment: $2200 (this is not a joke).

Areas to check out: You'll pay top dollar in hot areas such as the Upper West Side, Upper East Side, West Village, Hell's Kitchen and Chelsea. Try the East Village, Murray Hill, Washington Heights and Hudson Heights for slightly lower rents. Expand your search to Park Slope, Brooklyn, Roosevelt Island, Hoboken and Jersey City, NJ or Astoria, Queens and you'll pay less for more space.

Free resources:

Jakobsen Realty

www.nofeerentals.com (all sizes)

212.533.1300

William Gottlieb (West Village)

558 Hudson Street

212.989.3100

City and Suburban (Upper East Side)

511 East 78th Street (studios, 1 and 2 BR)

212.517.3000

Fannie Klein (Upper East Side)

1641 First Avenue (studios only)

212.570.6174

Pine Management Company (Upper West Side)

212.316.2114

Solil Management Company
212.265.1667

Sky Management
www.nofeeapartments.net
212.759.1300

Bettina Equities Management Company
www.bettinaequities.com
212.744.3330

Ardor New York
www.ardorny.com
(this is a broker with a fee but has some good deals anyway, sometimes with no fee)

Manhattan Skyline
www.manhattan-skyline.com
212.408.9447

Keyah (Upper West Side)
$20 (refundable) plus a business card will get you keys to go check out their apartments.
www.keyah.com
212.595.5565

Village Voice
www.villagevoice.com

Roommate Services:

Roommate Finders
www.roommatefinders.com

San Francisco

Overview: This one's another toughie. Check out Craigslist.org first and also consider expanding your search to the surrounding areas for a better deal.

Average price for a 700 square foot apartment: $1700.

Areas to check out: Noe Valley, Glen Park, Haight, UCSF, Bernal Heights, Mission. Commuting options for cheaper rent include: Berkeley, San Jose, Sunnyvale.

Free resources:

The Rental Source
www.therentalsource.com
415.771.7685

Affordable Property Management
www.apm7.com
510.487.2583

Ford Real Estate

www.fordrealestate.com

415.824.7200

Litke Properties

www.litkeproperties.com

415.922.0178

Saxe Real Estate

www.saxerealestate.com

415.474.2435

Roommate Services:

Rent Tech

www.renttech.com

Seattle

Overview: Not too cheap either, but you can get some good stuff online.

Average price for a 700 square foot apartment: $1200.

Areas to check out: Freemont, Ballard

Free resources:

Seattle Apartment Finder

www.seattleapartmentfinder.com

Roommate Services:

Rent Tech

www.renttech.com

Washington, D.C.

Overview: In town, you'll get a decent size space for a decent chunk of change. D.C.'s METRO goes everywhere, so don't be afraid to expand your search to Northern Virginia or parts of Maryland to see if you can get a better deal.

Average price for a 700 square foot apartment: $1350

Areas to check out: Northwest D.C., Dupont Circle, Cleveland Park, Woodley Park, Adams Morgan, Mt. Pleasant, Foggy Bottom, U Street, Capitol Hill. Try Alexandria, VA, Chevy Chase, Bethesda and Silver Spring, MD for slightly more space for your money.

Free Resources:

www.rentnet.com

A good place to begin you search. Lists management companies and offers direct links to apartments.

Charles E. Smith Company

www.smithapartments.com

Adina Kalish Neufeld

City Specific Furniture Finds

Chicago

Wolff's Flea Market
Corner of Mannheim and North Avenue
Melrose, IL
847.524.9590

All Night Flea Market
2015 Manchester Road
Wheaton, IL
Once a year extravaganza
715-526-9769

Affordable Portables Lifestyle Furniture
2608 North Clark
773.935.6160
www.affordableportables.net
Cheap and crammed in every corner of the store, lots of desks, tables, shelving, plus plenty of futons.

Brown Elephant Resale Store
3651 North Halsted
773.549.5943
Gently used furniture

Roy's Furniture Co.
2455 N. Sheffield Avenue
773.248.8522
Great deals on tables, chairs and sofas, with an enormous selection.

Room and Board
www.roomandboard.com
700 N. Michigan Avenue
312.266.0656
Very similar to Crate and Barrel, with some good deals on sofas. You can also find these in Denver, Santa Ana, CA and parts of Minnesota.

Crate and Barrel Outlet
800 West North Avenue
312.787.4775
Lots of cheap extras for an apartment, plus the occasional great furniture deal.

Los Angeles and Surrounding Areas

Out of the Closet
Some great bargains can be found at these thrift stores.
Locations in: Atwater Village, Beverly Hills, East L.A., Fairfax, Hollywood, Long Beach, North Hollywood, Pasadena, South Pasadena, Venice, Vermont, West Hollywood, West L.A.
323.860.5262

Further
4312 West Sunset Blvd.
323.660.3601
Sells funky new stuff.

Pasadena City College Flea Market
1570 East Colorado Blvd.
First Sunday of every month 6 a.m.–3 p.m.
626.585.7906

Rose Bowl Flea Market and Market Place
Second Sunday of every month
1001 Rose Bowl Drive
Pasadena, CA
323.560.7469

New York

Greenflea
Columbus Avenue and 77th Street
Sundays 10:00 a.m.–5:30 p.m. All year.
Forget the furniture, don't miss the cider donuts located at the corner entrance by the plants!

Hell's Kitchen Flea Market
West 39th Street between 9th and 10th Avenue
Saturday-Sunday 9 a.m.–5 p.m.
Lots of vendors have recently made this cool flea market even bigger.

ABC Carpet
www.abchome.com
Broadway and 19th Street
The place is mucho expensive, but you can get some fantastic decorating ideas—I list it for this reason only. There's also an ABC outlet in the Bronx worth checking out.

Gothic Cabinet and Craft
www.gothiccabinetcraft.com
Locations all over NYC

If you're willing to finish the pieces yourself, you can actually get a great deal. It'll cost you a bit more if you have them do it for you.

Straight from the Crate
212.579.6494
Locations all over NYC
Not dirt cheap but they've got a lot of space-saver options crammed into a small store.

San Francisco

San Jose Flea Market
www.sjfm.com
1590 Berryessa Rd.
800-Big-Flea
Wednesday-Sunday. All day.

Washington, D.C.

Eastern Market
www.easternmarket.net
7th Street and North Carolina Avenue
Saturdays 10 a.m. – 5 p.m.
You can find everything from jewelry to frames to furniture at this place.

City Specific Food Cooperatives (Co-ops)

Atlanta

Sevananda Food Co-op
467 Moreland Ave., NE
404.681.2831
www.sevananda.com

Boston

Harvest Co-operative Supermarket
581 Massachusetts Avenue
Cambridge
617.661.1580
www.harvestcoop.com

Chicago

Co-op Markets (Three locations in Chicago)
1526 E. 55th Street
773.667.1444
www.coopmarkets.com

Los Angeles

Co-opportunity Consumers Co-op
1525 Broadway
Santa Monica
310.451.8902
www.coopportunity.com

New York

4th Street Food Co-op
58 East 4th Street
212.894.3623
www.4thstreetfoodcoop.org
*Also check out the *Park Slope Food Co-op* in Brooklyn at www.foodcoop.com and the Greenmarket in Union Square (not a co-op but has great produce, breads and cheeses.).

San Francisco

Rainbow Groceries
1745 Folsom
415.863.0620
www.rainbowgrocery.coop

Washington, D.C.

Senbeb Co-op
5922 Georgia Ave., N.W.
202.723.5566

Chapter 2
Moolah
Getting yours in the right place

One of the most difficult things—maybe *the* most difficult thing about being on your own is managing your money. And even if you're not doing this 100 percent on your own, you're still going to be managing some of it (such as your daily cash flow, your expenses, your disposable income, etc.) in a way you've never had to before.

What's important to learn *goin' solo* is how to cut back. It doesn't matter how much you make either. Whether it's $20,000 or $100,000 a year, the key to financial success when you're just starting out is learning to live *below your means*. Yeah, I know . . . you're young, you're free, you have no mortgage, no kids and no responsibilities! Why save?

Because, if you do it now, you'll be better off in five years. End of story.

This was a very hard concept for me to grasp. My first job out of college paid $24,000 a year in New York City. I quickly learned that sushi and saki three nights a week, in addition to the astronomical rent for my minuscule apartment, wasn't the best way to get my money to compound. I weighed the options. Making my own sushi wasn't one, so I cut back. I stopped shopping for things I didn't need and I stopped taking cabs. I also went to Starbucks only on Fridays as an end-of-the week treat. And it worked.

So what does living below your means really signify on a larger scale for you? In talking with the experts, most suggest that saving 10 percent of whatever you make will do the trick. Think of it as your own little *tithe*. In biblical times, 10 percent of income (land or cattle) was given to the church as a gift. And while I'm all for donations, at this stage of your life it's best to donate your time and keep your money. I know what you're thinking (because I thought it too): "How in the world can I save 10 percent of my measly paycheck, which works out to, for example, only $1409.51 a month, after taxes?" Just pretend there are more taxes taken out and your check sucks even more than it really does.

I'm not saying deprive yourself of a fun night out, but don't blow $100 every Friday night and then wonder why you're not saving. Don't buy the new Banana Republic Harrison low-rise slate blue pin stripe pants for $88 (why everything there is $88 is beyond me) and then wonder why you don't have money. But I digress. The point is, starting early will make all the difference in the world. The best way to kick this process into gear is to take control of your spending. Here are some quick and easy suggestions that can help you do this without making you feel like a loser:

• Every now and then, put the four bucks you were going to use for a Double Decaf Mocha No-Foam Latte into a jar. You'll be amazed at how much you'll save by the end of a year.

• Go to the cheap movie theater instead of the expensive one (there's one in every city).

• Eat dinner at home and then go out for drinks, not both.

• Use your debit card instead of your credit card so money gets immediately deducted from your bank account. You'll be less likely to spend when you see your balance dipping into the double (or single) digits.

• Buy clothes off-season.

• Suggest doing holiday grab bags with your family so you only have to buy one gift instead of five.

• Avoid going to large dinner parties where everyone splits the check—even though you just ate a salad. It's easier than looking like the cheapo.

• Consider volunteering to be a guinea pig at a fancy hair salon. You'll get a great cut (or color) but you may not always get to pick the style.

Are you still with me? Living below your means is a challenge but every little bit helps. Start by following these suggestions and you'll gradually change your mentality to keep your spending habits under control. Put the money into a savings account until you can afford to open an IRA (Individual Retirement Account) and then have the money automatically deducted from your paycheck so you aren't tempted to do something else with it. Simply build your lifestyle around a reduced income for five years. If you need to, keep your money in a liquid account (one where you can withdraw cash with no penalty) in case you really need it.

What'll really help you control your spending is to set

a budget for yourself. Make sure it's realistic. Here are some things you'll want to include:

- Rent & Utilities
- Food
- Transportation
- Gas
- Cell phone
- Loans
- Credit card debt
- Gym
- Restaurants, Movies, Clubs, Leisure Activities

Based on this, add an additional 10 percent for savings and that's how much you'll need to make to survive. Or, log on to www.bankrate.com/brm/calc/worksheet.asp for an automated calculation.

Then, once you know how much you have to work with, you're going to need a place to put it.

Setting Up a Checking Account

This is something you'll want to do within the first few weeks of moving to a new city. If you're moving with a job, you'll probably get some advice from your employer along with a welcome kit from a bank. But if you're on your own, you'll want to shop around and see which bank offers you the most for less.

Some things to look for: Does the bank require a minimum balance? Does the bank charge a fee if you drop below the minimum balance? Is there automatic *overdraft protection* (an instant loan given to you by the bank if you take out more than what's in your account)? Can you link accounts? Is online banking part of the package? What's the fee if you don't use their ATMs? How many ATMs / branches do they have in the area? Do they have Saturday banking hours? What other services do they provide? There really is a difference between banks. Make sure you take a look at the suggestions listed at the end of the chapter.

Credit Cards

Most money gurus will tell you to avoid credit cards completely and stay out of credit card debt. They're right. But man, it's hard. Who can resist the extra 15 percent off at Banana (and Gap, and Benetton, and Abercrombie, and Ann Taylor) when you open a charge? But opening a slew of credit card accounts isn't going to help your credit and you'll likely lose them anyway. What you'll probably need, however, is a Visa, MasterCard or American Express. American Express offers fantastic customer service, but because vendors have to pay higher fees, it's not accepted everywhere. Just something to keep in mind. As far as Visa and MasterCard go, now that college is over, you won't get people yelling at you from tables in the student center with airline vouchers and free mobile minutes if you sign up. But there are plenty of cards out there that offer extras. Do a custom search for the best credit cards to suit your needs at www.bankrate.com (click on credit cards). Here, you can specify if you need a card with no fee, one with a low *Annual Percentage Rate* (known as APR— this is the amount of interest you pay each month if you don't pay your bill in full), cash back, or any that have perks and you'll get a detailed listing of a variety of cards.

One word of caution: a credit card offer may sound great on a brochure, but make sure you read the fine print on the back of the application. Many charge fees or have weird little clauses about when you have to pay up. This is especially true for those cards that invite you to "Transfer your balance" and "Pay nothing for five years!" Also, beware of introductory rates that advertise 0 percent APR. The fine print will tell you this only lasts three months and then guess what? You'll be paying late fees *and* a much higher interest rate. I learned this the hard way.

Student Loans

If you're going to start paying back any college loans immediately, you probably won't be able to save. But don't fret; getting out of debt is putting you in the right direction. If you have hefty student loans to pay back, now's the time to figure out how to do it and still have money left to pay the rent (and go shopping).

You've probably heard a lot about loan consolidation lately. So what is it? Loan consolidation allows you to combine two or more federal student loans together to give you lower interest rates, lower monthly payments and the ease of sending in one payment per month instead of several. Before you do this, figure out if it's worth your while. Many consolidation companies will market their services to you as if it's the perfect solution for your money woes. Once you combine your loans, you'll lock in the interest rate for the remainder of the loan period. This can be good or bad, depending on your rate. So do your research to get the best deal. "And," adds financial advisor Karen Schaeffer, "always figure out your budget *before* you decide to restructure your finances so you know what you're working with."

For detailed information on paying back your loans, log on to www.studentaid.ed.gov. For information on loan consolidation, log on to www.loanconsolidation.ed.gov or www.finaid.org. Karen also recommends www.myvesta.org, a not-for-profit consumer education organization. You'll pay a fee for the advice, but you'll get experts rather than people just working the phones who can help you figure out the best option for you.

If you do qualify for federal student loan consolidation, you'll have four options:

• *Standard Repayment Plan*:
You pay a fixed monthly amount for ten years.

• *Extended Repayment Plan*: You pay a fixed monthly amount for up to thirty years. Your interest will be higher even though your monthly bill is lower.

• *Graduated Repayment Plan*: You pay a low amount to start and then gradually increase your payments for a total period of twelve to thirty years. Your monthly payment will increase every two years.

• *Income Contingent Repayment Plan:* As it sounds, your monthly payments will be based on your personal financial situation. Payments are adjusted every few years. You'll have up to twenty-five years to pay back your loan.

No matter how you decide to pay back your loans, make sure to find out if you qualify for a grace period (where you don't have to pay anything for a few years), especially if you consolidate while you're still in school.

Some other words you may want to familiarize yourself with are *loan forbearance and loan deferment*. If you are temporarily out of work and have federal student loans, you may qualify to have those loans deferred until your financial situation improves. The government accepts the following reasons as grounds for deferment: unemployment; active military service; disability; full or part-time student. If you qualify, the government may also pay the interest for you. Contact your loan provider to find out what's best for you.

If you are in *loan forbearance*, you can hold off on paying back the loans for a set amount of time, but you'll be responsible for the interest that accrues. Still, while these options may work for you right now, it's always best to try and start paying back your loans as soon as possible.

If you don't even remember what kind of loan you have, log on to the National Student Loan Data System (www.nslds.ed.gov). Here you can search a central database of all Department of Education Loans and use their secure server to access your personal file.

Taxes

Just the thought makes me cringe. Like you really need to be reminded of your financial status when you're barely paying the rent? Taxes are a drag, but there's no way around them. You might as well take a deep breath and plow through this section.

Generally, if you work full-time for one company, don't have any side jobs or lots of money in different accounts, your taxes shouldn't be too crazy. You'll get a W-2 form in the mail (wage statements from your employer) and will need to fill out something called a 1040. If you make less than $50,000, you'll use the 1040E-Z or the 1040A (depending on your income and deductions). In addition to your W-2 forms, you'll get statements in the mail from your bank(s) or investment firm(s) listing interest you've made on your accounts over the past year. These are called 1099 forms. Since this interest is considered income, you must report it to the IRS. The income you get from working (called *earned income*) combined with income you get from your investments (called *unearned income*) makes up your *gross income*. You see this term a lot on your income tax returns.

Women *goin' solo* at twenty and thirty will generally file under "Single" (do they really need to remind you of *this* too? Geez!) and take the *standard deduction*. This is an amount of money calculated by the federal government that is deducted from your gross income (again, the combination of wages and income from investments). The whole concept of a standard deduction is based on the fact that the government knows you've spent money to further your career, make charitable donations, or pay medical bills, so they give you a break in a fixed amount. If you spent less than this—making résumé copies or doing something else you could deduct—consider yourself lucky, you get a freebie. If you spent more than the standard deduction, you'll probably want to *itemize*. This means you'll have to go through your receipts from the entire year and list out every business related expense to prove to the IRS that you indeed spent more on job-related things than what the government's giving you.

Things get a lot more complicated when you're self-employed, own your own business, work lots of different jobs or have money coming in from various channels. In any of these cases, you may need to file separate forms (known as *schedules*) to reflect income from these sources, be it contract work (for which you'll get 1099 forms from your employers) or dividends in excess of certain amounts. Additional information about schedules for businesses can be found in Chapter Five: *Entrepreneurs Take a Backseat to Nobody*, but here's a quick rundown of some that may apply to you:

- Schedule A is for itemized deductions.
- Schedule B is for reporting taxable dividends and interest income.
- Schedule C, Schedule CE or SE are for reporting profits and losses from a business.
- Schedule D is for reporting capital gains and losses.

If filing taxes is new to you and you've got income coming in from several different sources, I highly recommend getting an accountant, especially if you're planning on itemizing your expenses. Itemizing can get very nit-picky, as the IRS will want you to categorize your expenses accordingly. Ask around for a referral or stop by an H&R Block. The money you'll spend (their fee is based on the amount of paperwork you make them do) will be well worth it. A good accountant will make sure you get what's due you. And boy, does it feel good to get those piles of receipts off of your desk and onto someone else's!

When you're done with your federal income taxes, you'll also have to file tax returns for your state and possibly pay even more if you live in a city. That's right: more annoyance. To find out which state forms you'll need, log on to the Federation of Tax Administrators website (www.taxadmin.org) and click on Links and then State Tax Forms.

Accountant or no accountant, the key to getting your taxes done in a timely manner is keeping things organized. This means credit card statements in one folder, cash receipts in another, bills, bank statements and everything else all neatly labeled. If you ever get audited, you'll need to prove you spent and earned what you actually claimed. It's recommended you keep these receipts and bills in your file box for five years.

I have to give the IRS a little credit. They've made it easier to file, especially now that you can do it online at www.irs.gov. If you actually take the time and read the instructions on the forms themselves, you should be okay. Or, pick up the forms the old fashioned way at the library, local IRS office or post office.

Once it's all together, check over everything. Make sure you have all of the right forms included in your returns. Check to see that your address and Social Security number are accurate and that you've done your math correctly. If you have to pay, make sure you've made out your check in the correct amount and actually signed the thing! Don't forget to make copies of everything for your files.

I know it's so incredibly boring, but it is kind of empowering to do your own taxes.

Money Buzz Words

Even if you don't make enough to save, it's never too early to educate yourself on money and finance. If the only thing you do is curb your spending habits, get yourself out of debt and begin to read up on investment options, you'll be ahead. Think of yourself as a stock. You want to increase in value over time. Use this time to build a foundation and embark on your career. Your own net worth will go up because of what you yourself are becoming—a valuable asset to the work force.

When you're ready, take baby steps to Wall Street. I used to shy away from the whole money and investing thing because it just seemed too overwhelming. Bull markets, bonds, no-load, load—who needed it? I had no clue! So, before we do anything else, let's go over some commonly used market terms. Do whatever you want with these words, but at least be able to understand what they mean so that later you can use them to help you.

Stock – An ownership share in a company, which can be purchased by the public.

Bond – An instrument used to borrow money, maturing over a set period of time with interest, where the bondholder can cash in after the specified amount of time has ended. Remember those lame confirmation gifts you got from Aunt Ethel? Well, guess what? They're not so lame anymore.

Junk Bond – A high-risk bond with a low credit rating and a higher yield. I include this for no reason other than it sounds cool to throw around at cocktail parties.

Mutual Fund – A portfolio of individual stocks managed

by a professional. Mutual funds offer instant diversification, meaning you get shares of a variety of companies performing at varying levels which balance each other out, making your mutual fund a relatively safe investment. Fees will vary depending on how actively or passively the fund is managed.

Index Fund – A mutual fund made up of stocks attempting to mirror the performance of a major market index, such as the S&P 500 Index Fund. This is a group of 500 leading company stocks representing a wide range of industries. Index funds are a common choice for new investors because they offer diversification and low transaction fees. Losses from one stock will theoretically be balanced out by gains from another, keeping risk to the investor relatively low. Basically, an index fund is a fairly safe way to get market returns without following the market too closely. Other index funds include NASDAQ Index funds and Dow Jones Index funds.

Load – A commission paid on the purchase of a mutual fund price.

No-load fund – A mutual fund without a commission.

Money Market Account – A liquid account (one in which money can be withdrawn without a penalty) that offers a low interest rate and is generally used for short tem investments.

CD – Certificate of Deposit. A low-risk, low-return interest-bearing instrument which pays a fixed interest rate amount over a set period of time. A CD offers a slightly higher return than a Money Market Account.

Capital Gains Tax – Tax assessed on profits (such as money you make when you sell a stock).

Blue Chip Stock – A stock issued by a large, well-known company with a general record of solid performance.

Bear Market – An extended period of falling stock prices where everyone gets depressed and thinks they're broke.

Bull Market – An extended period of rising stock prices where everyone thinks they're rich and buys things they can't afford.

Dollar Cost Averaging – Investing a set amount of money in a mutual fund on a regular basis. This allows you to buy more shares when prices are lower, but you'll get fewer shares when prices are high, thus averaging your stock price so you don't have to worry about when to buy and sell.

IRA – (Individual Retirement Account) - A personal, tax deferred, retirement account to which an employed person can contribute annually.

Roth IRA – Established as part of the Taxpayer Relief Act of 1997, a retirement plan that allows taxpayers with certain income limits to contribute a set amount into a tax-free savings account. This is a great thing to set up through a discount brokerage firm if you don't have a full-time job.

401(k) Plan – A retirement plan similar in nature to an IRA, sponsored by an employer. Pre-tax contributions are taken directly out of your paycheck as an investment and many companies will match a portion of what you put in. Plans vary by company.

403(b) Plan – A retirement plan offered to employees of not-for-profit organizations similar to a 401(k).

Keogh Plan – A retirement plan for self-employed people.

Morningstar Inc. – A global investment research firm that helps people make educated decisions about their investments (stocks and mutual funds.) It's definitely worth your while to learn more about this company. Go to www.morningstar.com for more information.

Starting Your Portfolio

Don't laugh. Yes, you too can have a portfolio. Say it: "*Portfolio*"—sounds cool, doesn't it? Now pretend you're at a cocktail party "*Yes, I'm managing my portfolio*," or throw in the name of one of your friends—"*Matt Sanders is managing my portfolio.*" (I'm sure anyone out there with a friend named Matt Sanders is cracking up right now.)

Okay, now let's figure out what this means.

The key to successful long-term investment strategies is a *diversified* portfolio. You don't want to put everything into one company for obvious reasons (hmmm . . . can anyone say Enron?). And you'll need to keep some money liquid for different stages of your life, keeping your short-term goals (such as a car or grad school) separate from your long-term goals (such as a beach condo or your future kid's college fund). If you have a full-time job, you should invest in your 401K as soon as you're eligible. If you don't (or your company doesn't offer a 401K), open a Roth IRA as soon as you can.

A good place for beginners to buy an index fund or learn more about Roth IRAs is with a mutual fund family or a discount brokerage firm. Try and steer clear of firms currently under investigation for fraud. You may also want to look into *Exchange Traded Funds* (ETFs) which offer some of the same advantages as mutual funds but are traded more freely like stocks. To reiterate, index funds are a relatively safe way to start simply because one stock won't make or break your investment and you won't have to dedicate too much attention to following them. If you're only in it for the short term (less than five years), stick with a money market fund or CD.

Most financial advisors suggest investing in the stock market only if you're planning on staying with it five years or more. Hopefully in that time, you'll be in a better place to take a little more risk. Since investing is really about assessing your own tolerance for risk and possibly incurring some losses, if you know how much you can afford and how much of a hit you can actually tolerate, you'll feel less freaked out.

If you're really interested in learning more about money and investing, take a Saturday seminar or a continuing education class at your local community college. Here you'll meet lots of people like yourself who want to learn how to be smart about their investments but don't know where to start. The Learning Annex (www.learningannex.com) offers inexpensive classes in New York City, Seattle, San Francisco, Los Angeles and Chicago.

It's always worth reading up more on money matters, especially for women *goin' solo*. Here are some of my picks for the some of the better resources out there:

> *Smart Women Finish Rich: 9 Steps to Achieving Financial Security and Funding Your Dreams* (Revised Edition) by David Bach, Broadway Books.

> *A Woman's Guide to Investing* by Virginia B. Morris, Kenneth M. Morris, Lightbulb Press, Oppenheimer Funds, Bridget A. Macaskill, Mc-Graw Hill.

> Financial Muse – www.financialmuse.com. This website is chock-full of information on investing, brokerage firms and articles, such as *How to Pick Investments Based on Shopping for an Eggplant,* by money expert, Christopher Hayes.

Money Resources

Budget-Minded Banks

Washington Mutual – This bank is really making a name for itself nationally so I'll single it out. With over 2500 ATMs nationwide, Washington Mutual offers free checking with no fees and no minimum balance. Log on to www.washingtonmutual.com to find a branch near you.

Wachovia – On the east coast (from Florida up to Connecticut), Wachovia is another bank with new branches opening by the minute. They offer free checking with no fees and no minimum balance. Catch a promotion and you'll get to use other banks' ATMs for free as well. Log on to www.wachovia.com for more information.

Boston

Eastern Bank
www.easternbank.com
Branch locations:
101 Federal Street
265 Franklin Street
246 Border Street
Shaw's East Boston
Additional locations outside of the city
Number of ATMs: Over fifty branches outside the city with ATMs.
Basic Checking Account Rules: No minimum balance, no monthly service charges, free unlimited check writing, three free ATM transactions monthly at non-Eastern Bank ATMs.

Sovereign Bank
www.sovereignbank.com
Branch Locations: Too many to list.
Number of ATMs: Over forty-two around Boston.
Basic Checking Account Rules: No monthly service charge, no minimum balance, no per check charge, unlimited check writing.

Chicago

Mid America Bank Chicago
www.midamericabank.com

Branch Locations: Over fifteen locations in Chicago. Even more in the surrounding areas.

Number of ATMs: Plenty.

Basic Checking Account Rules: Totally free checking, requires no minimum balance, no per-check charge, no monthly service charge.

North Community Bank

www.northcommunitybank.com

Branch Locations: Over fifteen locations in Chicago metro. More in surrounding areas.

Number of ATMs: Over eighty.

Basic Checking Account Rules: The Freedom Account: free checking, $100 minimum to open. Direct deposit or minimum balance required for no fee.

Los Angeles

Wells Fargo Bank

www.wellsfargo.com

Branch Locations: All over

Number of ATMs: Lots and some of them talk!

Basic Checking Account Rules: Free checking with direct deposit, otherwise, small monthly fee.

New York

Amalgamated Bank

www.amalgamatedbank.com

Branch Locations:

15 Union Square

1745 Broadway

301 3rd Avenue

564 West 125th Street

Number of ATMs: Only at branches so while banking is cheap, this could be inconvenient if one's not near your place.

Basic Checking Account Rules: Free checking with no minimum balance, no monthly maintenance fee, no per check charge.

Independence Community Bank New York

www.icbny.com

Branch Locations:

250 Lexington Avenue

169 7th Avenue

43 East 8th Street

864 8th Avenue

Number of ATMs: Only a few at branches.

Basic Checking Account Rules: No minimum balance. No fees.

Chapter 3
So You Wanna Be a Doorman?
Practical ways to pursue a dream

Are you a dreamer? Answer these questions:

1. Do you sit at work thinking about ways to get out and follow your *true* calling (dancer, writer, actor, architect)?
2. Are you comfortable without a steady paycheck?
3. Are you able to structure your own day?
4. Are you good at setting deadlines and following them?
5. Do you always need someone to tell you what to do?
6. Are you one to follow the rules?
7. Do you take *no* for an answer?

Now, forget every question except the last. Those were meant to get you in the right frame of mind. If you answered "yes" for that question, then sorry, you're not a dreamer. Go back to your desk. For those of you who answered "no" for that question, this chapter is for you.

You're a dreamer. You're someone who can't understand the word *no*. Someone who'll do anything it takes to make your dream happen. This, of course, comes with a price. Dreamers often experience unimaginable lows: waiting for that callback, for the funding, for the editor to call, for the check to arrive—waiting, waiting, waiting. It's inevitable. Failure and waiting are inescapable elements of dreaming.

But just because you're a dreamer, doesn't mean you have to live in the clouds. There are plenty of ways to add practicality to your choices and help give yourself a little more of a foundation. Of course, first you have to decide what it is you want to do. Maybe it's opening a café. Maybe it's starting a band. Whatever it is, you must have a goal in mind. Then, prepare for everyone and their mother to tell you why you shouldn't pursue your dream. "It's too expensive!" "It's no life for an educated girl!" "There's too much competition!" "You'll never make it!"

Tell all of these people to take a hike. (For specific replies to pointed questions, see Chapter 7: *Dating Yourself*.) Set your sights on what it is you want and write it down. If your dream is to open a teahouse, you're going to need to research the ins and outs of tea. If it's to become an actor, you're going to have to find out about everything from headshots to training programs to monologues. If you want to become a writer, you'd better start writing. This chapter won't tell you how to do that. What it will do, however, is help you find ways to pay the rent, structure your day and stay focused while you're pursuing that dream of yours.

First things first—$$$. If you don't have this, it'll be mighty hard to compose your concerto.

Jobs For Dreamers

Generally, dreamers require flexibility for their dreams to come true. You may need to keep your days open for auditions, lunch meetings or classes. You're still going to need a steady cash flow but you don't necessarily have to be stuck in an office from nine to five. While we all know about the waiter and temp thing, there are plenty of other unique and flexible jobs that offer a solid paycheck too. Are you a night owl? Do you have trouble waking up in the morning? Best to get a "day job" that lets you sleep in. Just leave some time to schedule your plan of action. The following alternative choices might be just what you need to feel good about yourself while you're on your way.

Doorperson

You won't be able to do this if you're not in a big city, but if you are, here's the scoop: The average doorman makes $25,000 a year and works approximately four eight-hour shifts a week. But wait! During the holidays, most tenants give between $25-$100 each as cash tips, depending on the building. An apartment building with two hundred apartments will add around $15,000 in cash to your salary. The job is mostly unionized, can be very competitive and doesn't always get the best rap, but if you're willing to work off hours, you could make a decent living while you're shooting your independent film. In New York log on to www.seiu32bj.org for an inside look at the building services unions and additional contact information.

Another option is that of concierge—a higher end doorperson / information specialist. This is a bit more professional in nature—some cities will make you take a test or even show a license. You'll need to have stellar customer relations skills. A good concierge can command fantastic tips and is well sought after. Sound intriguing? Check out The National Concierge Association at www.conciergeassoc.org to learn more.

Dog Walker

Like dogs? Why not take 'em for a walk at $10 a pup. Walk one three times a day and that's $30. Walk ten three times a day and that's $300 a day. Robyn P. started doing this and eventually left her job as a secretary to start her own pet sitting business in New York City, walking an average of five dogs a day at $25 a pooch. "You can easily make $1000 a week in this business if you work on your own," she says from her Upper East Side apartment. "It's all about taking a risk and doing something you believe in."

If you want to be like Robyn, you'll need to spend about $300 on bonding and licensing insurance, get your name out there (local newspapers, posting ads on bus stops and community centers are all good places to start) and really love animals. Robyn suggests working for a company first to learn a bit about the business before going out on your own. Afterwards, you'll probably be able to command as much as $30 for every half-hour walk (if you walk one dog at a time as opposed to a pack of ten). If you specialize in personalized doggy attention (baths, grooming, etc.), the clients will pay you more.

For information on how to become a professional pet sitter, contact the National Association of Professional Pet Sitters at 800.296.PETS, Pet Sitters International (www.petsit.com) or the National Association of Professional Dog Walkers (www.napdw.com). This job is more lucrative in big cities where there's no yard for Rover. If you live in Chicago, check out Central Bark (www.centralbarkchicago.com). In New York, try Central Bark West (www.centralbarkwest.com).

Fact Checker

This is one of the best gigs in the publishing biz. Nab a job at a magazine as a fact checker and you're in. What is that you ask? A fact checker is someone who's responsible for verifying the factual content of a feature article or news story. Every quote, every statistic, every lush lash mascara price, every spelling on the Swedish do-it-yourself hair removal kit *must* be verified before it's published. You know how some writers make up quotes to sauce up a story (and we're not just talking tabloids anymore)? Well, the fact checker nips that in the bud by making sure the quote is accurate. It's tedious work and one that requires serious attention to details. You'll be on the phone a lot. But it's important work and one that will truly sharpen your research skills. For around $20 an hour, you'll also get the inside scoop on everything that goes on inside the magazine or newspaper biz. Some publications are a little more flexible than others. Some will even let you work from home. This is also a great way for writers to meet editors. Contact the research department at any magazine or newspaper and inquire about fact-checking opportunities. If they're looking for someone, you'll have to take a quick test to make sure you know the difference between primary and secondary research, as well as information about pop culture, gardening, politics or whatever the subject of the publication. Once you land the gig, you're pretty much in and can make the rounds to other publications through word of mouth. Companies like Hearst and Condé Nast run a slew of magazines. If you can nab a fact checking job at one of these places, you'll stay busy.

While there are fact checking opportunities nationwide, your best bet is in New York City, as that's where the most magazine editorial offices are.

Computer Doctor

If you're really skilled with computers, you may want to consider offering your services to help those who are technologically challenged. Generally the rule is as follows: The more powerful the executive, the more technologically challenged she is. This means that every head honcho out there is basically clueless when it comes to computers. Set up a little Computer RX business and post signs around town and in the local papers. Make your services easy to understand so as not to confuse the clients. Try this: *Computer Doctor at Your Service. Your body needs a check-up? Your car needs a tune-up? Save yourself angst and money before your system crashes and you lose everything! Reasonable rates for the following services and more: Cleaning up Hard Drives, High Speed Consulting, Upgrading memory, Fixing any little annoyances, No Job Too Small!* You get the point.

Tutor / Substitute Teacher

Go fish out your old SAT scores. Did you get anything near a 700 on either section? If so, call up your local Stanley Kaplan, Princeton Review or SCORE Prep office and sign up to be an SAT and college prep tutor. The hours are extremely flexible; you'll usually work in the afternoon when school gets out or in the evenings. The hourly fee starts at around $15 to $20 if you work for a company, but can skyrocket to over $200 an hour depending on your specialty. On your own you'll probably make a little more cash but you'll have to find your own clients too.

For a steadier source of income, you may also want to consider working as a substitute teacher or teaching English as a Second Language (ESL). One writer summed it up nicely: "Subbing is the best freelance job I've ever had." Why? "You're done by three p.m., it's well respected on the résumé and will broaden your scope, the money's great (typical pay in the Northeast starts at $80 a day—a little less in the Midwest and on the West Coast) and you can set your own weekly schedule." But don't think it's gonna be a breeze. "Being a substitute teacher does not equal a free and easy work day," says freelance writer John C. "You are expected to follow a thorough lesson plan which the teacher leaves for you and to interact with students regularly, not just sit there." While you won't work in the summer, you can use this time to tutor kids too. If you opt to be a full-time substitute, you'll be on call all the time but you'll also get medical benefits. For most part-time substitute teaching positions, you'll need at least an associate's degree (a BA will get you a little more money), a clean record and a sealed, official copy of your college transcript.

If you live in Chicago, check out After School Matters (www.aftershoolmatters.com). Here, you can teach a course for after school programs on a technical or creative topic.

Personal Assistant

Be prepared to kiss a lot of A★★ here. But, you'll also make heaps of contacts. If you get in with the right person, you can make a load of cash, enjoy some perks of celebritydom and possibly have time to develop your own interests. Administrative, organizational and networking skills are a must. Working as a personal assistant is not for everyone. It may allow for some flexibility, but you'll *always* be at the beck and call of your employer (day, night or right in the middle of something really important). Make sure and ask for references from previous personal assistants so you don't get stuck with a tyrant. A good place to start is by consulting the Public Relations Society of America (www.prsa.org) website. Just so you know, it's a very competitive field, so use your networking tactics to get in (see Chapter Four: *Opening the Door*). There are also professional organizations like New York Celebrity Assistants or Los Angeles Celebrity Assistants that can help you begin. Whatever you do, just don't start wearing sunglasses indoors.

Real Estate Agent

Real Estate brokers in big cities (both rental and sales) can make a lot of cash, especially when the market's hot. A typical rental broker's fee in cities like New York and San Francisco can run anywhere from 12 to 15 percent of the *annual* lease. Sales fees run the gamut, averaging around 6 percent. In the first chapter, I told you how stupid you are if you pay a broker's fee for a rental—but hey, if you can't beat 'em, join 'em! If you like looking at apartments and houses, if you're aggressive (real estate is another *very* competitive industry), if you consider yourself a people person and have a flair for selling, then real estate might be just the career for you. Look online for "real estate courses" in your area or contact a few agencies to find out what they require. Some agencies may also pay for your license if you're lucky. And another great perk: you'll have access to hundreds of apartments before anyone else, especially in the most competitive markets.

VICTORY!

Cynthia B. came to New York to make it as an actress. Instead of landing a job at the local café, she decided to take a crash course in real estate. She shelled out $299 for the class at the New York Real Estate Institute (212.967.7508), another $50 for her real estate license (renewable every two years) and got a job at one of the largest apartment brokers in Manhattan. Now a senior rental agent, Cynthia typically works for a few months at a time, averaging ten to fifty hours per week and then takes a break to work on her acting career. "It keeps my energy up and allows me to focus on what I want, when I want." Last year she worked for ten months and made $70,000 without missing an audition. No clock-ins and no schedules—everything on her time. Most importantly, she doesn't sit around all day waiting for a callback. "It makes getting rejected from an acting job not so bad when you look forward going to your day job. I can pick and choose what I want to do. And the best part about it is I'm making money and I feel good about myself."

Personal Trainer

Do you spend a lot of time at the gym? Are you really "into it?" Then maybe you should think about becoming a personal trainer. First, you'll need to get licensed or have a degree in exercise physiology. With this, you can get a job at a fitness center, as an in-house corporate trainer or even take on your own clients. The going rate is vast, spanning from $30 to $500 an hour depending on your experience (and number of cool Spandex outfits). Contact the American Council on Exercise (www.acefitness.org) for information on getting certified. Then, get crunchin'.

Tour Guide

Every city needs good tour guides—or as one put it: "A concierge on wheels." If you have a great memory, know your history and like talking, this job is for you. Prepare to memorize a tremendous amount of facts. Language skills come in handy too. You're going to deal with lots of different kinds of people and be asked to take a ton of pictures. Being a tour guide is not only a fun way to make money, it's also a great way to make contacts. For actors, you'll get a chance to practice your audition skills. The hours are as flexible as they come and the pay starts at around $8 an hour plus tips, in major cities like Chicago, Boston and New York. If you're really into giving tours, think about museums, theme parks, theaters and other attractions in your city that may be looking for guides. Here are a few bus companies to get you started:

Boston Duck Tours: 617.723.3825
Chicago Duck Tours: 800.298.1506
Gray Line New York City Tours: 212.445.0848
Starline Tours of Hollywood: 800.959.3131

Personal Shopper

If you like to shop and know your stuff, call up your local department store and inquire about personal shopping opportunities. You'll need to have retail experience and stellar interpersonal skills—this is a real customer service oriented position. Higher end stores, like Nordstrom for instance, even require a portfolio, filled with photos of outfits and hot looks you've put together for clients (or your roommate, but don't tell). Once you land a job as a personal shopper, you'll exercise your trendy talent finding anything from articles of clothing to accessories for a variety of folk. It's also another good way to make contacts. While most department stores offer full-time positions (Bloomingdales, Saks Fifth Avenue, Marshall Fields, Nordstrom, Robinsons-May all have personal shopping departments), hours can be flexible and you may be able to work nights and weekends. Salaries range from $25,000 to over $100,000 depending on experience. Higher end stores work solely on commission.

Charlene G., a personal shopper in Atlanta, recommends spending lots of time in the store getting to know the lines. "This can be an extremely lucrative business if you know fashion," she says. Charlene typically works thirty hours a week, enabling her to pursue a second career as a fashion stylist. "You can do anything you want if you put in your time, get out there, meet people and network. It's kind of like running your own business." She also notes how important it is to dress well. "You're representing yourself out there, so it's best to look good at all times." A personal shopper's service is usually free, so you don't have to be a hard salesman, just someone who knows and loves trends.

Another type of shopping you may want to try is Mystery Shopping. Here, a company will hire you to scout out the competition of a product or service (or even test out their own clerks' customer service skills) and you'll be paid to report on your findings. You can make some good cash mystery shopping if you hook yourself up with the right company.

Trade Shows

You can make a killing working trade shows, which come in all shapes and sizes. From huge technology expos in major cities to regional shows in small towns, companies are always looking for upbeat, well-spoken presenters or demonstrators to showcase a product. If you're good at memorizing scripts, smiling and repeating yourself one hundred times a day, you may want to tap into the trade show market. Most every major industry offers trade shows, the biggest and most fun (not to mention the free stuff you'll come away with) are Toy Fairs, Technology Shows, Boat Expos and Food and Gift Shows. Generally, a trade show will last around four to five days and will require you to know the company's product inside out so that when the trade show floor is opened, you'll be there ready to demonstrate their wares to the throngs of people stopping by the booth. You'll repeat the same speech until you're blue in the face, be on your feet the entire time and drop dead on your bed each night from exhaustion. But, the pay is ooooh, so good, with lots of travel opportunities. A seasoned trade show demonstrator can easily make between $3500 to $5000 in four days—if not more. The bigger the show, the more competitive the sales team, the more money's in it for you. The trick is getting your first trade show.

If you've got the spunk and the personality, try calling the corporate headquarters of a bunch of toy companies and ask the receptionist how to get in contact with the people who handle the trade shows (like Toy Fair). Do the same for technology or motorcycle companies. Remember, there's a trade show for every industry out there. You may have to make a few calls before someone helps you, because there's no real clearinghouse for these jobs—although the marketing department is a good place to start. An Internet search in your industry of choice will give you a list of vendors you probably never knew existed. Call as many as you can and then follow up with a professional cover letter and headshot (if you have one) along with a current résumé.

Religious Education

You hated going as a kid, but did you ever think you could actually make money doing this? It's an easy way to express your creativity with kids, who frankly, are sick of school and need some innovative means of education. Jody P. moved to Chicago and immediately contacted a few synagogues while she was looking for a full-time job. Because she held a bachelor's degree and had some experience speaking Hebrew, she got a job teaching three afternoons a week. For $35 per hour, at six hours a week, she was able to bring in some quick cash and interview at her own pace without feeling anxious about money. She also tutored some of her students on the weekends for $50 an hour. Contact your local church or synagogue and inquire about religious school teaching opportunities. The best time to do this is late summer.

Clown / Party Character

This is a great side job for actors. Look in the telephone book or on the web under "Children's Parties." Many companies who organize these events hire freelance clowns, Nemos, Elmos, Cinderellas, (or any other character that's hot) to spend an hour or two entertaining kids at birthday parties. It'll test your improvisational skills and it's a lot of fun. The pay ranges from $30 to $50 an hour plus tips. Christmas is also a great time to contact party planning agencies for company holiday parties.

Catering

There's nothing like a free gourmet meal. You're sure to get this when you work for a caterer (although you may have to sneak under the table to eat it). The work is tiring and the hours are long, but the time will pass quickly. Kitchen staff makes an average of $8 to $12 an hour while servers can get upwards of $15 to $40 an hour, plus tips. From Bar Mitzvahs to weddings to company picnics, there's plenty of work to go around. Contact caterers in your area and inquire about temporary work. Make sure to say you've done this before, even if you haven't. It's a little secret that worked for me.

Flight Attendant

This may not be the most flexible job in town, but it sure gets you where you want to go. Stick with the flight attendant biz for a while and you'll work your way up the seniority ladder where you can pick your flights. The average pay for a flight attendant isn't fabulous—it starts at around $15,000 a year—but you may also get expenses and *per diems*, depending on the airline. Most flight attendants work an average of seventy-five hours per month so you can still have some time for yourself. Says seasoned flight attendant Kiki W., "So many airline personnel begin second businesses simply due to the amount of time off, so it's a great way to supplement another career." Kiki's been flying for American Airlines for almost twenty years and still loves the job.

Some things to keep in mind: You must have good vision, be at least nineteen years old, fit the height and width requirements (they don't measure weight anymore) and have a U.S. passport. The more flexible you are in terms of living, the better. One writer found working as a flight attendant was the best way to work on her travel book—without paying a dime for the travel.

Club Promoter

This is a job for very social types. As a promoter, your job will be to create a buzz about a particular bar or club and attract hot, hip people to the venue. You'll get a percentage of the cover charge for the evening, so the more people that show up to the bar or club, the more money in your pocket. Most promoters work by sending e-mails, passing out flyers, networking with friends and talking to DJs and club owners.

For a list of clubs and nightlife in New York, Boston, Philadelphia and Washington, D.C., in addition to occasional job postings, check out www.joonbug.com. In New York City, try www.impulsenyc.com.

Housekeeper

Some hate cleaning. Others find it therapeutic. If you fit into the second group, consider working as a part-time housekeeper. It's not glamorous, I know, but you can work on your own time, listen to your own music and make some easy cash. Maybe you specialize in home offices, maybe you only do studio apartments. Get yourself a gimmick and post a few signs around town, on bus stops, or place an ad in the local paper and send e-mails to your friends at work. You can easily make $100 a day cleaning two apartments and even more for offices. Again, you gotta like to clean, but if you do, why not make some money while you're at it?

Odd Jobs

To take the housekeeper thing one step further, are you handy? Maybe you know how to set up DSL like no other. Can you split a cable wire and run it through an entire apartment? Perhaps you know how to hang curtains, build shelves or lay carpet. Whatever your skill, market it. This is something you can do on your own time. Post a few signs around town and put an ad in the local paper. A good handywoman is hard to find. You can charge per hour or per project—your pick. Do a little research to find out the going rate in your area.

Videographer

Are you in film school? Do you have access to a digital camera? If so, why not market your skills as a party videographer? You'll need to be somewhat business savvy for this and you'll probably need to know about editing too—most clients want a finished product. But hey, if you're in film school, you probably know how to do it anyway. A skilled wedding videographer can make anywhere from $2500 to $5000 an event, depending on the coverage necessary.

These are just a few options to help you. If you're really going to pursue that Broadway career, you're going to need to carve out time to do it. If you can't handle being a waiter, find something else. That way you can call yourself a *consultant*. It will make you feel better when people ask you what you do. The most important thing is to stay positive, no matter what you're doing. Making money is a great way to do this. But remember, you're going to have to work hard to make it happen.

But What About Health Insurance?

Yeah, I know. Not too many of these choices offer full time benefits, such as a 401K and health insurance. But they do offer flexibility. So, you'll have to find your own. One plus for those who're self employed: you may be able to deduct 100 percent of your health insurance on your tax returns. See, there are more advantages to *goin' solo* than you thought!

Here are a few choices to consider if you're on your own:

• **Ehealth Insurance** – For a comprehensive listing of different plans around the country and a free online quote, log on to www.ehealthinsurance.com .

• **Catastrophic Insurance** – Ask your health care provider if they offer Catastrophic Insurance plans. These can range anywhere from hospital coverage only to more comprehensive services and will likely come with a much higher deductible. So, while you won't pay a huge monthly fee, you'll get charged more if something happens to you. Use this as an absolute last resort rather than going without any health insurance at all.

• **Membership Organizations** – If you're a member of a union (such as the Writers Guild (www.wga.org), the Screen Actor's Guild (www.sag.com), the Authors Guild (www.authorsguild.org) or any other for that matter), you may also qualify for their health insurance plan. If you're self-employed, contact the National Association for the Self Employed (www.nase.org) and see what's available to you. For those living and working in New York City, check out the Freelancer's Union at www.workingtoday.org. Here, you'll find lots of information about health insurance policies for those *goin' solo*, as long as you're working an average of twenty hours per week.

Health Insurance Terms You Should Know Before You Shop Around

Deductible – The amount you will pay out of pocket each year to visit a doctor or go to the emergency room before your health plan kicks in.

Premium – The monthly fee you will pay for service, whether you get sick or not.

Cap – The highest amount you'll have to pay for any one year of coverage.

Co-pay – A fixed amount you pay to your doctor each time you visit.

Pre-existing Conditions – Any illness you had before you signed on with an insurance company.

Network – A group of doctors who participate in a particular health plan.

Out-of-Network – Doctors who don't participate in a particular health care plan. *Note, just because a doctor is out-of-network doesn't mean you can't see her. You just may have to pay more out of pocket.

Types of Health Care Plans

With so many plans available to the consumer, here's a breakdown of some of the most common:

• **Fee-For-Service** – This is where you pay a percentage and the health insurance company pays a percentage. Generally these plans allow you to go to any doctor but you'll also have to file your own claims.

• **HMO (Health Maintenance Organization)** – There's usually no deductible and a small co-pay but you will have to see a primary care physician each time you get sick.

• **PPO (Preferred Provider Organization)** – Similar to an HMO, but your choice of doctors will be much larger. You may incur a higher per-visit co-pay.

• **COBRA** *(Consolidated Omnibus Budget Reconciliation Act of 1985)* – Extends a company's health coverage plan to former employees (and their families) for a set period of time after their employment has been terminated. The former employee is responsible for paying a monthly fee for continued coverage, which, by the way, can be costly.

Questions For Your Provider

Once you do get someone from a health insurance company on the phone, here are some questions you should ask:

1. What plans do you offer for individuals?
2. What services are offered under each plan? Make sure

to ask if your plan covers specialists. If you're planning to visit the dermatologist monthly, you want to make sure that this is included. Also make sure to ask about preventive health care, birth control and immunizations.

3. Is there a *cap* on fees in a *Fee-For-Service* plan? If you choose this type of plan, which doesn't have a deductible, make sure you ask this question.

4. Do you offer a *non-cancelable policy?* This means the provider will continue to cover you as long as you pay the monthly premium.

5. Does your policy cover *pre-existing conditions*?

Spend some time asking the agent to explain everything in detail, even if you have to ask the same questions over and over. This stuff is really confusing but you want to make sure you understand your policy.

Back To The Dream

Oh, yeah. Almost forgot. Now that you've conquered the paycheck and your health insurance, it's time to focus on the dream again. Easy to get lost in the money stuff, isn't it? One of the most important decisions you're going to have to make involves being honest with yourself. Are you really able to handle rejection on a regular basis? If not, pursuing your dream may be more difficult than you'll ever imagine. Generally, the more creative the career, the more difficult the process. Since there are no rules for pursuing a dream, you'll have to just keep plugging away. Whether it's pitching articles to editors, auditioning for plays, testing new recipes, or trying to land an agent, you have to have tunnel vision. Make sure you get the right kind of side job that allows you to continue to pursue your dream, otherwise you'll just get caught up in the job and forget about what you're really trying to do.

Choosing the Right Dream Job

What is it that you love to do? Think about it. Now think about your personality and how it suits your goal. If you're a recluse and simply can't talk to people, no matter how hard you try, you're probably not going to land a job as a publicist, movie producer or press agent. Maybe you're better suited as a writer. On the other hand, if having no one to talk to all day gives you suicidal thoughts, then a job as a freelance writer isn't the best choice for you either. You'll need thick skin to make it on Broadway. If you don't have people skills, you probably won't make manager of the year. So, yes, it's important to pursue your passion, but it's also important to be realistic with your own personality and your own limitations with regards to that passion. Some people are more driven than others. Some people take bigger risks than others. Some people have more natural talent than others. Where do you fit in? Maybe you want to be a writer but need a steady corporate income. A good compromise could be working as a corporate writer. Try not to romanticize your profession. No matter how great somebody else's successful career seems, chances are, there was a lot of hard work involved in getting there. Whatever it is you choose, you'll have to dedicate as much time as you can to your pursuits. Be realistic with yourself and you'll get there faster.

Managing Your Time

Managing your time efficiently requires a lot of dedication. This holds true whether you've got all the time in the world to follow your dream, or you're working a full-time job and pursuing it on the side. Organization is key. Some people may even find it harder if they have all the time in the world because then they have to structure their entire day around, well, nothing! Whatever situation you find yourself in, you'll need to do the following:

• *Set deadlines and goals* – This will force you to stick to a schedule. Your monthly calendar should include practicing your craft at least three times a week for starters. If you have to wake up at five a.m. to draw your designs, then do it. Make it a Monday, Wednesday, Friday ritual. It's really easy to blow this off. But if you have a goal written on a calendar, you'll be more likely to stick to it. It's also helpful to tell people about your goals and ask them to remind you when the time comes to show them your progress.

• *Allot a certain time of day to your dream every day* – Knowing you have from six a.m. to eight-thirty a.m. to write will help you stay focused. It may be difficult setting your alarm an extra hour or two early, but if you have to be at work by nine, you're going to need to carve out your own "dream time." In your head, your "dream planning" should be just as important as the job you're getting paid to do.

• *Take a break* – Don't get too frustrated if you're not meeting your pre-set deadlines. Take a look at your schedule.

Have you tried to cram too much into a month? You won't be productive if you're not honest with yourself. Better to take longer than to try to rush to get something done.

• *Don't let your relatives get you down* – Everyone wants their parents to be proud of them. But unfortunately, not everyone's relatives are supportive when informed their beloved "A" student wants to move to Hollywood. You'll get a better response from your family if you have a plan laid out (i.e.: how you'll pay your rent without begging them for cash)—but you should still be prepared for some resistance. After all, they've invested a lot in you—why aren't you going to law school? Stay focused, positive and practical and they'll eventually get it.

• *Stay Fit* – Staying fit will help you adhere to your schedule. Feeling good about yourself and your body will allow you to release energy so you can stay focused. You don't have to spend a bundle at an expensive gym either (see some gym listings at the end of the chapter). Look for deals at local community centers where you may not get fluffy towels and spa shampoo but you'll get the same results. And don't forget the free stuff that's right outside your expensive door!

Surviving Rejection

How will I ever face the world again? How many more times am I going to have to do this? Maybe I should have gone to law school; Mom was right, this is no life for an educated girl. Let's see, I've probably uttered these phrases oh, at least a thousand times? Surviving rejection is a must for dreamers. Why? *Because the more you dream, the more you'll be rejected.* Take that for what it is and you'll already be one step ahead of the competition.

Now, what can you actually *do* about it? Here are some of the ways I've picked myself up off the floor. Use whichever ones work for you:

• *Use rejection as a tool* – for every rejection letter you get, send out five more queries. For every audition you mutilate, go on five more. Make it a rule. If you let one measly bad day or one fool get you down, how will you play in the big leagues? Make a collage out of your rejection letters. I made wallpaper out of mine.

• *Work it off* – Get a rejection letter? Do ten crunches. No, make that twenty. You'll feel even the slightest bit better.

• *Cry* – Rejection sucks, so it's okay to feel sorry for yourself. Cry and kick and scream and say it's not fair. Call someone and whine—but don't call the same person every time. You need to ration the number of people who listen to you complain.

• *Surround yourself with people who understand* – Find a group of people like yourself who are all going through a similar experience. You'll discover there are plenty of others who are dealing with the same ups and downs. Share your war stories with each other and have a few laughs. You'll feel better.

• *Eat Chocolate* – This is a must. But only do this after step two.

• *Buy yourself a rejection treat* – Don't spend a lot here—you can make yourself feel better with the smallest little gift. Get yourself a manicure or a new hat. Don't do it all the time either, since you'll be buying something every day (I did and it wasn't good) but every now and then you're allowed.

• *Get over It* – The more you wallow, the more time you waste. Remember that rejection is part of the game, so if you want to stay playing, you're going to have to learn to be resilient.

Some Final Thoughts on Being a Dreamer

This world is filled with competitive and talented individuals. Be relentless about your goals and you'll eventually make it. You may not make it in the way you had originally anticipated, but something will happen. Really.

VICTORY!

Cameron S. of Boston, MA had just given birth to her first baby when she realized her dream of being an aerobics instructor wasn't going to be so easy. Not satisfied with staying at home all day and unable to afford daycare, Cameron took her baby and started an aerobics class for new moms. The catch? They had to bring their babies to class, stroller and all. A stroller pushed back and forth up a small hill not only rocked the baby to sleep, but offered a low impact workout for moms wishing to shed some of their pregnancy weight. Six reps of lifting baby up and down created a sea of giggles from the tots and also toned their moms' biceps. Cameron used her noodle to make great money from a unique business. And although she can afford it, she doesn't need daycare anymore.

City Specific Fitness Rejection Busters

Cheap Gyms

Chicago

Lincoln Park Fitness

2342 North Clark

773.281.8715

A bare bones one-room gym, but the monthly fee is pretty cheap, plus there's no registration fee.

Webster Fitness Center

www.websterfitness.com

957 W. Webster

773.248.2006

A fun gym that claims to be the cheapest around and the "last of the neighborhood clubs."

Lakeview YMCA

www.lakeviewymca.org

3333 N. Marshfield Avenue

773.248.3333

Much more than you'd expect, with a four lane pool, cardio and weight rooms and racquetball courts.

Irving Park YMCA

4251 W. Irving Park Road

773.777.7500

Indoor heated pool and loads of classes.

Absolutely Free in Chicago

Lakefront Running Path

Runs from the Northernmost part of Lincoln Park South through Grant Park and down to the Museum of Science and Technology in Hyde Park—an eighteen mile trip.

Lincoln Park

From North Avenue to West Hollywood Avenue, between Lake Shore Drive and Clark Avenue, this park has space for biking, Rollerblading, running, softball and kickball. There's even a chess pavilion. Cross-country skiers can also be found here in the winter.

Los Angeles

24 Hour Fitness

www.24hourfitness.com

One of the cheaper gyms in town with branches every-where. Make sure you sign up for the free trial!

Center for Yoga

www.centerforyoga.com

230 ½ N. Larchmont Blvd.

323.464.1276

Offers very reasonable rates on classes in L.A.

Absolutely Free in L.A.

Grant Park

From Randolph Street to Roosevelt Road, between Michigan Avenue and the lakefront, Grant Park has over 300 acres to explore, including tennis courts and softball fields.

Topanga Canyon State Park

Miles of beautiful trails for hiking and biking.

Beach

This one's a no-brainer. Some special spots include Zuma Beach in Malibu and Leo Carrillo State Beach, just before the Ventura County line.

Griffith Park

Over fifty miles of hiking and biking trails, plus picnic areas, tennis courts, a golf course and playgrounds.

New York City

Lenox Hill Neighborhood House

www.lenoxhill.org

212.744.5022

70th Street between 1st and 2nd Avenues.

One of the best bargain gyms in NYC. A small weight room but it has a great pool. Fees are dirt cheap.

Dolphin Fitness Clubs

www.dolphinfitnessclubs.com

These bare bones gyms are open 24 hours in select loca-tions around NYC (mostly on the East Side).

McBurney YMCA

125 West 14th St.

New York, NY 10011

212.741.9210

Offers classes galore as well as a huge pool. You'll pay less here than at most NYC gyms.

Absolutely Free in NYC

Hudson River Parks

Recently extended, this path now stretches all the way from Battery Park to beyond the George Washington Bridge on the West side of Manhattan. There are also kayaking and rowing piers along the way.

Central Park

More beautiful than ever before, you can spend the day Rollerblading, biking, horseback riding, jogging, hiking, boating or just lying in the grass of this 800+ acre oasis in the middle of New York City.

East River Walk

Follow this path all the way from 63rd Street along the East River up to somewhere in the 120s. Stop at John Jay Park, Carl Schurz Park and even Gracie Mansion, once home to many NYC mayors, but now an historic city site.

Chapter 4
Opening the Door
How to network with confidence

Networking. The word alone sounds intimidating, but simply put, networking is the smartest way to get *anything* you want. It's about being in the know, gathering information and finally, meeting the people who can help get you where you want to go. Whether it's scoring an inside tip on an apartment, finding a guy you might actually want to date, or securing a job interview, networking is the way to do it. Someone once gave me some very useful advice. While interviewing me for a job, she asked me to describe the best way to network in five words or less. I couldn't answer so I sat there looking like a lost sheep. "Turn one person into five," she said sternly. I didn't get the job but I never forgot that rule.

The thing to remember about networking is that it exists everywhere. Andy Warhol once said that everybody is a potential client. Just because someone doesn't look the part, doesn't mean she doesn't have the goods. Some of the best contacts are made by simply saying "hello," even if you're on a bus ride in the middle of nowhere. You just need to relax and open your mind to a new conversation. Don't be afraid to *schmooze* a little.

Networking Events

These things used to make me so nervous I wanted to throw up. It felt like a competition to see who can gather the most business cards—all while clutching a cell phone, martini and Kate Spade tote. They come in all forms: cocktail parties, dinner cruises, alumni functions, basketball games, weddings, bar mitzvahs and even funerals. Still, as intimidating as they are, they work. Sometimes you need to fake it and play the game. If you're really dedicated to making networking a part of your life, you might as well try out a few of these things. It's kind of like going to the gym. You may get nothing out of it at all, but at least you can say you went. Sooner or later, you'll see a few networking muscles develop. The more you do it, the better you'll get. Once you're at a networking event, here are some useful tips in mind:

• **Don't Sprint to the Buffet Line** – Nobody wants to shake your hand while you're balancing a plate of shrimp and cocktail sauce. First of all, it'll seem as if you're more concerned with filling your stomach than meeting people. The buffet line is really a diversion—it's somewhere to go when you're taking a *break* from the crowd. Grab a stuffed mushroom here, take a piece of Brie there, but don't walk around with a heap of tortel-lini. It's not becoming. Instead, focus your attention on who you want to meet and why. Yeah, I know, it's easy to look busy standing by the food. I used to do this until I realized I wasn't gaining anything except for a few extra pounds. You're allowed to hold a glass of wine. It'll give your hands somewhere to go.

• **Conquer Your Fear** – Take a deep breath and go introduce yourself to at least two new people. Be honest, direct and as confident as you can without being phony. It's difficult—in fact, really difficult—but try saying something simple like, "Hi, Mr. X, I'm Robin. I really admire your work and was wondering if you had a few minutes to give a novice some advice about the x industry." I know it sounds stupid to practice, but it helps if you stand in front of the mirror.

• **Do Your Homework** – Call the sponsoring organization beforehand and find out who's going to be at the event. If you had to register to get in, chances are the attendees will be known ahead of time. Other times, trust your intuition. If you think someone is a person worth meeting by the way she looks or her general aura, go with it and introduce yourself. If she's not the VP of HBO, then at least you've challenged yourself to make an introduction. And just maybe, you'll meet a new friend.

Something else to keep in mind: "It's really helpful to know a little about the person with whom you're talking," says Karen McGee, Director of Career Services at Syracuse University's Newhouse School of Communications. Try doing an Internet search on the individuals or companies. Find out what their most recent projects were, their latest campaigns, any current news, bios, etc. Give yourself some ammo to bring to the event. It will feed your confidence and make you stand out in a conversation.

• **Read Up** – It's really important (make that *imperative*) to know as much as you can about the industry you're trying to break into. Trades, daily newspapers, magazines, online sources—the more you know the better. Try to make reading part of your daily routine, even if it means getting up an extra thirty minutes earlier than usual. You'll feel empowered and have the tools you need to get ahead. A great way to do this without shelling out cash for subscriptions is to plop yourself at the library or favorite bookstore and read.

• **Act Your Age** – Nobody likes a poser. If you're trying to get into medical school, don't pretend to be a doctor. Be informed and be knowledgeable, but don't try too hard to impress unless you really know your stuff. Better to ask lots of questions rather than to try to come across as having all the answers. People will see right through you if you don't.

• **Don't Ask for a Job; Ask for Advice** – Try a little tact here. People love talking about themselves. Use this tool to its fullest extent. Questions like "How did you get your start in the business?" and "Tell me about your background" open the door for a longer conversation. Immediately jumping to "I'm looking for a job" puts someone on guard and makes him think you're only out to get something. Networking is about building long-term personal relationships. You may not get immediate satisfaction, but good questions and timely follow-up will help you immensely in the long run. Be suave. Don't be a Nervous Nellie. But don't waste your entire evening in a long-winded conversation with someone you're not really interested in either. If you find someone pontificating too long about the "good ol' days" of college or his particular industry, thank him for his kind assistance, say you don't want to monopolize his time and move on. Now's a good time for that shrimp.

• **Dress Appropriately** – Going to a tailgate party? Stay away from the business suit. Going to a cocktail party? Black works. Try and gauge the event and the industry it's for. That way you won't stick out like a sore thumb or feel ill at ease. Also, wear something you're comfortable in. It's no fun tugging at your skirt for the entire evening or worrying that your new hot pink bra is showing. Don't go nuts spending money on clothes, either. Instead, buy one "networking outfit," something sharp, and one "interview outfit," something a little more professional. If you feel good in what you're wearing, you'll have an added sense of confidence.

• **Be Assertive** – This is perhaps the most difficult aspect of networking—asserting oneself without being too annoying. Remember, your goal is to get information that will help take you to the next step. This might not mean getting an interview immediately, but it may lead you to the person who will get you there.

If you're talking with someone for a while and finding it productive, don't be afraid to ask if you can call her to talk further.

Questions like: *Is there someone you know who might be willing to talk with me? What professional organizations are you a member of? Would it be okay for me to give you a call next week?* are good ways to get people to open their Rolodexes for you.

"Know what you have to offer," adds Karen. Remember that you have skills too and a good employer is always on the lookout for new talent. If you sound wishy-washy you won't make a strong impression. Be able to answer the question "What skills do you think are your strongest?" with gusto. If you want to be a graphic designer, then say that. Be as specific as possible. Confidence sells.

• **Learn How to Shake Hands** – Shaking hands is an art. A strong, well-shaken hand leaves a lasting impression. The converse is also true. Shake hands like a limp fish and there go your brownie points. The goal is not to cut off circulation, but to be firm, confident and secure. Practice with your friends.

• **Always Repeat a Name** – This is one of the quickest ways to build your own list of contacts. Don't overdo this, but as soon as you meet someone, repeat her name. Do it at the end of your conversation too.

• **Make Sure you have the Right Tools** – If you're going to a true networking event, you should bring an updated résumé and a business card that has your name, phone number and e-mail to leave behind. Keep it simple. You don't have to spend $500 investing in a graphic designer. Look online at places like www.businesscards.com or go to Staples. For around $20, you can design your own. www.vistaprint.com offers free business cards if you let them advertise on the back.

Another big must: make sure your résumé is accurate and up to date. Don't say you were an executive producer if you were a production assistant. Very bad.

• **Let Jerks be Jerks** – There are plenty of them out there. Some come in bully forms. Others just don't give a hoot. Recognize that not everybody is out there to help you; most aren't. Every now and then you'll meet a genuinely nice person who'll give you all the time in the world. The people who're in a position to help you are usually very busy. Recognize this. But your time is valuable too. If you feel someone's jerking you around or trying to lure you into something not right for you, say a polite thank you and continue on your merry way.

• **Pay Your Dues** – Sometimes the only way to get your foot in the door is to intern. You know—work for free, volunteer—call it whatever you want. It doesn't matter how many degrees you have or how old you are. The more competitive the career, the more likely it is you're going to have to put in your time without pay, at least for a while. Suck it up and give 'em your best shot. Ask if there are any volunteer opportunities (even if a company isn't hiring) and then structure your work schedule around it. This will show you're willing to do whatever it takes to get your start. If you're good, you'll probably get noticed in less than six month's time.

• **Not Sucking Up** – While we're on the subject, let's talk about sucking up for a minute. There's plenty of room for flattery and compliments, just make sure they're genuine. If you lay it on too thick you'll be viewed as transparent. Kudos are fine when they're deserved. You can say you like the way someone handled a client, or even that you like her haircut, but just don't do it every day. One exec said he was so disgusted every time a particular intern came to a meeting because the intern dispensed compliments left and right and had no sense of when to stop.

• **Don't Get Discouraged If You're Not the Queen of Schmooze** – If it were easy, everybody would do it. If you're shy, that's okay. Shy people can have great conversations. Try to get into smaller groups rather than larger ones where you won't feel dominated. A one-on-one conversation utilizing the same tactics will get you just as far. Be brave and keep practicing. Force yourself to go to at least one new event a month. You'll be surprised at how well you'll do after a few of these. Try practicing on new people you meet at a dinner party or on an airplane.

• **Follow Up** – You must follow up with every single networking contact. This is just as important as making the contact itself. You should do this within twenty-four hours of meeting someone. If she doesn't immediately return your call, don't give up. If you tell someone you met at a party that you're going to send her a writing sample, do it right away. She might forget about you if you wait too long. Also, short hand-written notes are a great way of saying "It was nice meeting you!" and add a personal touch when you aren't sending anything official. Making the contact is only the beginning, so don't let your hard work go to waste.

• **Relax** – Networking is all about talking to people. Are you a people person? Do you like learning about others? Are you *remotely* interesting? Then you have nothing to worry about! Go in, feel confident and knock 'em dead!

VICTORY!

Marianne M. graduated from Syracuse University at a time when nobody was hiring. Determined to get a job in film development, she researched fellow S.U. alums at the career center and came across the name of a top producer. After reading in the trades that he had recently been promoted to VP of Production at New Line Cinema, Marianne took a risk. She picked up the phone and called his office. Coincidentally, he picked up his own line. She introduced herself and told him simply that she had called to congratulate him on his recent promotion, "from one S.U. alum to another." That's all, nothing more. Impressed with her drive, he asked her what she was up to, as he now needed an assistant. Could she fax over her résumé and references immediately? Several conversations later, without ever meeting Marianne in person, he hired her over the phone. Within seventy-two hours she packed up her stuff from her parents' house in Delaware, moved into a hotel in Los Angeles and started work the following Monday. Now she's reading scripts, handling appointments and working her way up the production ladder. All because she took a chance.

Schmoozing Scenario

The Set-Up

You just happen to be sitting next to the director of marketing at Miramax films at your friend Rodney's wedding. As soon as you find this out, your knees start shaking. You knew she'd be there, but sitting next to you? And so we arrive at a perfect networking situation. You've wanted to work for Miramax since college but nobody has responded to the hundred-and-one résumés and standard cover letters you've already sent. You tried calling once but you hung up when the receptionist answered for fear of sounding stupid. Well, now's your chance, so don't blow it!

When to launch into the conversation:

Timing is key. You don't want to look like you're only there to network. This is a social event. You're having fun, remember?

You've just returned to the table after a sweaty round of

the *Hora* so you're adrenaline is pumping. Now's the right time to meet-and-greet. The bandleader has just requested that everyone return to their tables. "The salad is being served," were his exact words. Nothing like a little schmoozing over some radicchio. Introduce yourself. Just do it. Put your hand out and say: "Hi, I'm Emily, it's a pleasure to meet you." She'll most likely return the handshake. If she doesn't, you have a major problem. So now, go ahead and try this:

> YOU: "I'm really glad Rodney seated us together. I've heard a lot about you."
>
> HER: "Really, I don't know squat about you."

Okay, maybe she won't say this, but she'll likely say something to the effect of "Really?" while wondering who the heck you are.

> YOU: "I've always been a huge fan of Miramax. I hear you just optioned "x".

Here's where your strategy comes into play—you should know something about the company and which projects were recently acquired. You know this from your weekly reading sessions at the bookstore.

> YOU: "I read that the writer worked for six months on a farm to get a better sense of how to write from the perspective of a cow."
>
> HER: "That's pretty funny. I actually didn't know that."

You've just informed an exec of something she didn't know without doing it in an annoying way. Nice work!

> YOU: "Have you been with the company a while?"
>
> HER: "About fifteen years. I started in the mailroom and then worked on up to director of marketing. It's a great place."

The goal now is to get her to ask you what you do. If you're lucky, she'll say something like: "By the way, what do you do?" *but more likely, you'll probably sit quietly for a moment and have to launch into it yourself. What the heck. Take a deep breath and keep talking.*

> YOU: "Right now I'm freelancing (*try to use words like* freelancing *or* consulting—*it sounds better than temping*) for a few different places in their marketing departments. I do mostly copywriting and I love it. But I'm always looking around."

You're keeping it real here. You don't want to look like you hate what you do. That'll make you less marketable.

> HER: "Well, I wish I could say we're hiring right now, but it's not happening. Sounds like you're doing some interesting stuff though."

Don't freak out—it's not over. This simply means she can't offer you a contract right here and now, next to the dinner rolls. Keep the door wide-open.

> YOU: "I'm sure it's tight everywhere now. I actually just finished a project for *xx* and I'm working on *yy*. But, I'd love to send you some writing samples. Would it be okay if I popped something in the mail to you?"
>
> HER: "Sure, why not."

After the salad . . .

At this point you've gotten up and down a few times to dance. The Chicken Cordon Bleu is being served. Try to loosen the conversation up a bit so you're not only talking about work.

> YOU: "How long have you known Rodney?"
>
> HER: "I met him after graduate school in blah, blah, blah."

You don't really care how long she's known Rodney; you're just getting her to open the door for you to throw in some humor and to deepen the personal connection. She doesn't need to know this. Now's a perfect time for a personal story.

> YOU: "Did he ever tell you about the time that his mother caught him with Jeanette in the laundry room?"

You don't have to really dig up something rude here (especially if she's a relative!), just something funny and memorable. I can't help you with this one.

Later that evening . . .

> YOU: "It was really great meeting you, NAME. (*Always repeat a name*). Oh, before I forget, let me get your address so I can send you those writing samples. I almost forgot!"

This is you trying to sound blasé. You've been waiting for this moment since the salad arrived. Just sound like you almost forgot—you'll seem less desperate. Make sure you have a pen tucked away inside your beaded handbag and then grab a cocktail napkin from the bar. Very Hollywood.

> HER: "Great meeting you too. Give me a call."

Bingo. You got the info. Now it's up to you to follow up. And you didn't even want to go to Rodney's wedding.

Cold Calls

There's a reason these things are called cold calls. They're icy, they're awkward and they can really make a girl shiver in her boots. Maybe that's why sales jobs pay such high commissions.

Cold calls suck. But you still gotta make 'em, no matter what industry you're in. It's just part of the game. The key is to keep doing it. Here are some tips to help you get over the fear.

One Word: *Assistant*

The assistant is just as important as the person you're trying to reach. Knowing this is the key to successfully getting to the people you really want to speak to. She can be your best friend if you know how to talk to her. Whether assistants like to admit it or not, they're gatekeepers—the people who can make your life miserable or blissful, depending on their mood. Assistants have their own issues with power and sometimes the only way to express it is with people on the phone. Your job is to *empower the assistant*—to make her feel as if she's the important one, because eventually she will be. Treat the assistant like dirt and you won't get anywhere, fast.

I once sent a query letter for a film script directly to the assistant after talking to her for over an hour about my idea. I asked her honestly what she thought and if she'd like to read it. I didn't even mention the name of the producer. I knew the assistant would pass it on if she liked it, so I wasn't concerned. When I finally sent a letter to the producer outlining my idea, it was two months later. And guess what? The assistant now was the producer! I was in the office with her for a meeting a week later.

Generally, the assistant is the one who reads everything first. If she doesn't like it, your query letter or résumé won't even make it to the next level. So, if you're making a cold call, talk to the assistant for a while. Tell her what you're looking to do and ask for *her* advice.

Now, if for some reason you actually get the head cheese on the phone, you'd better be prepared to sell yourself and do it quickly. Your main points should be addressed within the first few seconds of the conversation: *Your name, How you got to her, Why you're wasting her time*. After you get these points across, you'll get a general idea of how she's going to respond. Most likely, you'll get some sort of an insipid reply—meaning she's probably doing five other things at the same time. Don't let that deter you. Keep your spirits up and ask her if it's okay to send her something in writing outlining your plan. A cold call followed by a note is the best way to keep your name fresh in someone's mind. Finally, always end the conversation with the goal of getting to the next step: Is she willing to meet with you? Can you call her in a few days? Is there something specific you can send? Would she rather receive it via e-mail or snail mail? The key is to do whatever you can to ensure that there *is* a next time.

Writing Strong Queries and Cover Letters

Marcy H. receives over three hundred cover letters a week. An editor at a major publishing house in New York City, she usually tosses 75 percent of them. Same goes for the hundred-fifty queries a week that Meg J. receives for film script ideas at her agency in Los Angeles. Bottom Line: *Most unsolicited letters and queries get thrown away.* Now this doesn't mean that 15 percent are still viable, but it's best to use your personal contacts to get in. Even with a personal connection however, a strong cover letter is imperative. This is not to deter you from sending unsolicited mail, just be prepared not to hear anything if you do. The best way to get your letter on someone's desk is to do the following :

• **Always Get a Name –** You can bet that a "To Whom It May Concern" letter will get tossed first. Why? Because it's just too darn hard for people to figure out where it's supposed to go. The harder you make it for the people in the mailroom (or an assistant who opens the mail), the more likely you'll fall into the black hole. Always get the *name* and *title* of the person you're looking to impress. Then address the letter directly to her. Make sure your spelling's correct. If possible, call her assistant and let her know you'll be sending a letter of introduction, even if there's no job posted anywhere.

• **Have a Purpose –** Nobody wants to scan a letter to figure out why you've written. Even if it's just to introduce yourself and let someone know how much you want to work for the company, make it clear. Cover letters and queries come in all shapes and sizes, with the more creative industries requiring a bit more innovation, but the most effective ones in all categories address the following points:

1. Introduction
2. Purpose of your letter
3. How you can help the company
4. Timeline of activity
5. Conclusion

Think of your cover letter or query as a mini-business plan. Here's a sample of a simple but strong letter from someone looking to be a research assistant for a magazine with no current job openings:

Dear X:

I am a recent graduate of the University of Wisconsin with a degree in English Literature and a minor in French. I am writing to express my sincere interest in Research Assistant opportunities at *xx Magazine*. As an avid reader of xx, I am especially interested in your *Health and Wellness* section. While working as a reporter for my college newspaper, I learned the value of meticulous research by writing and fact checking my own pieces as well as those of my peers. I am skilled at mining information from primary sources to support an article and am relentless at seeking just the right experts to offer quotes in a particular area. While I am aware that there are no current openings with your division at this time, I hope you will keep me in mind for the future. Enclosed is a current résumé and clips for your review. In addition, I would be most interested in coming in for an informational interview at your convenience and will follow up with a phone call in several weeks. I certainly appreciate your consideration and look forward to learning more about xx's research department.

Thank you very much for your time.

Sincerely,

Sign your name

Type your name

Polishing Your Interview Techniques

Think about all the people you know who handle themselves well in public: great communicators, charmers, politicians, even people you meet at dinner parties. You can immediately tell when someone's engaging because they've just "got it." Generally, successful interviewees come across as *genuine*, *interested* and *interesting*. This means they've got something unique to add to a conversation; they've got a certain style of presentation and they're good listeners. All three of these qualities make for a good interview. "And," adds Ronit F., a Senior Human Resource Manager in New York, "don't forget to do your homework!" This means researching as much as you can about a particular company before you get in their office. Knowing the market and the business is a sure way to impress. Chit-chat is fine but keep it short. "I don't want to hear about your nephews," says Ronit, "no matter how cute they are." Also, I shouldn't have to mention this, but dress appropriately. If you think your skirt is too short, then it probably is (unless you're applying for a job at Hooters). Keep an upbeat positive attitude and stay interested, no matter how boring the interviewer may be. And don't chew gum or wear too much perfume. You don't want to be remembered as the Chanel floozy.

You should always come equipped with examples of how you handled yourself in previous work situations. For the most part, interviewers are pretty standard. They'll ask you something like *Can you give me an instance when you dealt with a difficult work situation? How did you handle it?* Think about these types of questions beforehand so you don't get caught off guard. And bring samples of your work in a clean binder. Finally, no matter how hard it may be, you must ask questions! This doesn't include "What's my salary and when do I get a bonus?" Intelligent questions about the company's policies and practice, departmental responsibilities, future developments, etc. will give you a better picture of the position and let the interviewer know you're truly interested. Always come prepared with a few smart ones. Even if you're not the least bit interested in the job, pretend as if you are the entire time. While this job might not be the right fit for you, the interviewer may know of something else that is.

Dealing with Strong Personalities

They're out there all right. And they come in every shape and size: small, tall, fat and thin; the quiet intimidators and the outright bullies. Sometimes you just have to listen. An interview is not the time to get confrontational, so don't let your ego get in the way. If you find yourself in an interview situation where you're being intimidated, your best bet is to try to read the person as best you can and give him the answers he wants to hear. There's a reason people act like bullies—they're insecure. And insecure people need to be reassured. Make them feel powerful by giving them the right answer. You'll have to be able to gauge this on your own. But you'll also have to make a decision right there whether or not you want to work for this person.

I once worked for a film producer who pretty much made me feel like crap. She was a true terror and her movies, well, they didn't get too much critical acclaim. So, she acted like a tyrant as a way to express her power. After I was able to rationalize this to myself, I could separate her tactics from my feeling bad about myself. I learned an incredible amount from her (especially about how *not* to run a business) and eventually left the job. But she always liked me because I was able to feed her what she needed to feel important. It's a tough thing to do, but here's where politics really come into play. The more despotic a person you work for, the more you're going to have to suck it up during the day. Just think of all the great stories you'll have to tell your friends at night.

Interview Follow-Up

Had a great interview but haven't heard from anyone in two weeks? You sent the *typed* thank you note (yes, there is a difference); now it's time to get on the horn. Pick up the phone and call. Express your interest in whatever it is you went to interview for and ask what their time frame is for hiring. Don't wait for them to call you. This is another opportunity to be proactive. This is especially true with creative careers. If you're calling to update an agent on your acting career, you should have something new to say each time you call, such as an invitation to a showcase of your work or a recent booking you got on your own.

Question: *But how do I know the difference between persistence and annoyance?*

Answer: Be able to read people. If you're truly calling with new information about yourself or your project, then you're not being annoying; you're updating them. But if you're just calling to say "hello" and nothing more, hoping they'll cast you in their next film, then that's a waste of time.

Handling Job Rejection With Grace

It happens to the best of us—getting canned. You think you aced the thing and then you get a form letter three weeks later. Well, you may not be able to do anything immediately about it, but if it's a job (or a company) that you really, *really* want, you might as well give it one last try. If you're curious to know why you didn't get the job, then pick up the phone and ask. Also, you may want to write a nice note to your interviewer, explaining how you were disappointed that you didn't get the job and hope to be kept on file if the needs of the company should ever change. This is a classy move. You'll be remembered for this and you may just get a call in a few months time. It's also a great way to keep the lines of communication open.

> **Remember the Golden Rule of Networking:**
> *Turn One Person into Five*
>
> If you meet someone who you feel can help you move in a particular direction, get five more names from that person and follow up with each one. Whether it's a friend, a business contact or someone you meet at the bank, if you follow up on all leads, you'll eventually wind up with a fat Rolodex of resources.

Once You Get the Blasted Job

Hopefully all this networking, cover letter writing and cold calling will pay off sooner than later. If you get a job, congrats! It's well deserved. I won't spend too much time telling you how to move up the ladder, because by now it should be obvious. Quickly though, the best way to impress your boss is to do the following:

- Get there before her and stay later than her.
- Don't engage in office politics.
- Keep away from negative people (it will rub off).
- Accept the fact that there'll be menial tasks associated with your work and do them with a smile (even if it's fake).
- Be friendly toward your fellow coworkers.
- Stay up-to-date with your industry.
- Make suggestions and volunteer for new assignments.
- Every now and then, when you feel like your job sucks beyond belief, take a deep breath and say to yourself: "I'm putting in my time. I'm putting in my time."

Additional Networking Resources and Job Info

Events, job boards and listings, cocktail parties, seminars, films, contacts— you name it, these companies and sites know what's going on. Check 'em out. Also, make sure you're accurately listed in your college alumni database so you'll get all the mailings. Don't forget to sign up for regional events too.

www.womenforhire.com – Lists information on networking events and career fairs.

www.digitaleve.org – Non-profit organization for women in new media, technology and communications with local chapters in Chicago, Houston, Los Angeles, Philadelphia and Seattle, just to name a few.

www.witi.com – Women in Technology International hosts networking events all over the globe and offers information to support women working in technology.

www.mediabistro.com – Posts articles, resources and great discussion boards as well as comprehensive job postings for media industries all across the country.

www.staffingthecity.com –Temporary positions specific to creative, marketing and administrative jobs in the Chicago area.

www.npo.net – The web site for Chicago non-profits jobs, where you can find lots of positions in the communications industry.

www.chicagojobs.org – Provides great links to support groups, job fairs, mentoring programs and job sites.

www.hollywooddigest.com – Has a list serve for screenwriters and filmmakers.

www.ifp.org – Non-profit service organization supporting independent filmmakers.

www.wif.org – Women In Film hosts networking breakfasts, lectures and workshops.

www.winm.org – Women in New Media offers information, resources and networking events for people in the New York area.

Chapter 5
Entrepreneurs Take a Backseat to Nobody
Do you have what it takes to start a business?

Your friends all tell you your orange crumb muffins are to die for. People come for miles to taste your Key Lime pie. And even though you're sending out résumés for big banking jobs, secretly, you're wishing you could open a bakery. We talked a lot about dreaming in Chapter Three: *So You Wanna Be a Doorman*, but opening a business is a lot different than pursuing a dream. Unlike writers or other trades which can be practiced from home, an entrepreneur needs to have a space (and insurance, and a license and employees) to fulfill her dream. And this translates into money. If you've always wanted to open a business or you're unemployed and getting frustrated with the dearth of jobs in your line of work, maybe it's time to really think about what it means to become an entrepreneur.

According to the Center for Women's Business Research in Washington, D.C., the number of privately held women-owned businesses in the U.S. has increased by 14 percent over the past five years, currently standing at around 6.2 million firms. "Many people will venture out on their own at an economic downturn," says Radwan Saade, Regulatory Economist at the Office of Advocacy for the U.S. Small Business Administration in Washington, D.C. The real question is however, how long will they stay there once the economy picks back up?

Well, that depends on what kind of businesswoman you are.

Is Entrepreneurship for You?

Entrepreneurship isn't for everyone. Owning a business and not having to answer to higher-ups may sound glamorous, but success doesn't come without a price. Some aren't sure if it's always worth it. "I'm married to my job," says Candice R., a small gift shop owner in New Jersey. "I eat, sleep and breathe the business. Sometimes it's just not worth the anxiety." Be prepared to spend most of your time working. You'll have to serve as your own secretary, mail clerk and press agent right away, so you should be comfortable wearing a lot of hats. Like the dreamer chapter, here are some questions you may want to ask yourself before you even think about starting your own business:

1. Are you able to structure your own workday or do you need someone telling you what to do?
2. Can you handle (both physically and mentally) the uncertainty of not always getting a paycheck every month?
3. Do you have a business plan?
4. Are you comfortable working alone?
5. Have you checked out the competition for your business?
6. Do you have a realistic picture of how you're going to execute your business?
7. Do you know how to market your business?
8. Do you have money put away to help get your business of the ground?

The Business Plan

A business plan is useful no matter what you want to do. Basically, it's a guideline that details your plan of action and shows you know what you're talking about. If you'll be seeking funding, you'll need one of these, no matter how small your business. It'll help you stay organized and be more realistic about your goals. Though many may differ according to industry, they'll basically include the same components.

I. Introduction – This is the first section someone will read, so you need to make it eye-grabbing. If you're looking for funding to open a restaurant, your first few sentences should explain to the reader why your restaurant is going to be the best one in the neighborhood (and not just because your parents'll eat there!) If you're trying to pitch a book idea to an agent, the introduction should sell the title, the concept and the author (that's you). Note: if you aren't a writer, then hire a professional to help you produce a business plan. It's worth every penny.

II. Your plan of action – Here's where you write the nitty-gritty details of what, exactly, it is you'll be doing and how, exactly, you'll be doing it. Who will your business target? Where will it be located? What's your unique product? How will it be used in the market? Writing this section will force you to think realistically about your goals in terms of execution.

VICTORY!

Helga W. of Greenbelt, MD felt the heat immediately after 9/11, when she was laid off from her job as Vice President of a top communications firm in Washington, D.C. Instead of sending out a horde of unsolicited résumés and cold calling potential employers, Helga took a hard look at the market and decided to challenge her industry. "I realized the PR world was affected greatly. Clients were no longer going to spend big budgets on their accounts," she says from her newly created home office. Along with a few colleagues from her firm who'd also been let go, Helga formed *Missionworks*, a Public Relations firm specializing in not-for-profit and corporate public interest accounts. Immediately they shaved money off the top by each agreeing to work from home. "This allowed us to pass the savings on to the clients, giving us an ability to stay on top of the competition," she says. Helga admits it took a while to get used to the change of lifestyle. She cut back on high rent and commuting fees by moving from the city into the suburbs. But being away from the action was a challenge and forced her to read more in order to stay up-to-date with current trends. Since opening its doors in 2002, Helga's client list at *Missionworks* has grown at a slow but steady pace. Helga's advice to women embarking on their own businesses is short and simple: "Start off with a six-month reserve so you don't starve, work hard and recognize that you probably won't turn a profit for at least two years. Always charge an upfront fee, no matter how small. And learn how to write a business plan—or pay someone to write one for you."

III. Market Analysis – This is where you show that you've done your homework. You'll need to study your market to find out what's already out there. Are there comparable businesses where you're looking to open up? Have there been other books on the same subject published recently? Remember, investors will look for any possible reason to say "no" to your project. The biggest reason for a rejection is usually because it's already been done. Be prepared. Defend yourself against being turned down by knowing what the obstacles are and how you'll overcome them. List the comparable products or services in your area. Then briefly write a sentence or two about why your idea is different.

IV. Marketing and Promotion – Do you have contacts

at *The Today Show*? Can you get yourself in the local paper? Anything you can do to help sell your product or service using the media is important to include in your business plan. Publicity sells. If a casting agent sees that you can get yourself into media outlets, you'll make her job easier. It's up to you to figure out how you're going to publicize your biz. Don't wait for your customers to find you. Figure out what strategy works best for you: Direct mail? Paid advertising in local media outlets? Flyers on cars? Screaming on the street corner? There are plenty of ways to be creative without contacts.

V. Timeline for Your Business – Investors will need to see that you've got a plan of action. "I want to open a dance studio one day" is not a plan of action. A month-by-month calendar of your plans (even if they never come to fruition) is. You must demonstrate you're truly embarking on the process if you want people to believe in you. Scouting out locations, realtors, monthly expenses, projected opening dates, costs, etc. should all go into your timeline. Depending on the nature of your dream, you may or may not need something more formal in terms of a spreadsheet. This is where your Microsoft Excel tutorial will come in handy. Leave absolutely nothing to the imagination. In fact, try and think of every possible question someone may have about your plan—especially if you're asking for money upfront. The more you can answer these questions before they're asked, the better position you'll be in.

VI. Sample of Your Work – Whether its sample chapters from a book or a portfolio of your best photography, anyone giving you money will ask to see what you've done. Make sure it's the best representation of you.

VII. About You – This is where you make yourself look pretty—very pretty. On paper that is. Write a bio about yourself, what you've accomplished, where you've been. The more you can include about your accomplishments, the better. But be honest. If you weren't the president of your sorority, don't say so. It'll come back to haunt you.

VIII. Summary – Here's your final chance to "sell it." Combine everything you've just outlined into a few neatly written paragraphs. This is your closing argument.

For additional help writing a business plan, check out the following books:

Business Plan Kits for Dummies (with CD Rom), by Steven D. Peterson and Peter E. Jaret, For Dummies.

Adams Streetwise Complete Business Plan: Writing a Business Plan Has Never Been Easier! by Bob Adams, Adams Media Corporation.

Next Steps

Registering Your Business

Are you embarking on this challenge alone or do you have a partner? Different types of business arrangements require different forms and legal documents. You'll probably fit into one of the categories below.

Type	**Sole Proprietor**
Definition	For those truly *goin' solo*. You'll be the only one responsible for all aspects of your business.
Pluses	Easy to set up. You simply need to register your name and get started.
Minuses	Yep, you are the one solely liable for all aspects of your business.
Some Tax Forms You'll Need	Individual Tax Returns (1040) Schedule C or SE –Self Employment and Profit or Loss Tax, State and local business and sales tax.

Type	**Partnership**
Definition	An agreement between two or more people. Should include a breakdown of ownership, division of profit, intended length of partnership, compensation and procedures to follow should the partnership be dissolved.
Pluses	You aren't the only one responsible for keeping the business thriving. And you don't have to divvy up the profits to outside investors.
Minuses	Can get sticky if you don't have an attorney draft a legal agreement. Don't leave anything up to chance or a good friendship can go sour. Each partner can be liable for

the other partner's action done in the name of the partnership.

Some Tax Forms You'll Need	Form 1065 (Partnership Income) and / or 1065 K1 Schedule SE – Self-Employment Tax Form 1040 – Individual Tax Return Schedule E – Supplemental Income or Loss. State and local business and sales tax
Type	**Corporation – C Corp**
Definition	Decisions about the company are made by the largest shareholder or the board of directors.
Pluses	Can raise money by selling shares of the company.
Minuses	Can be costly to set up and maintain. Records must be kept on everything and often times, the president of the company must answer to the board of directors, or stockholders. *A lawyer is highly recommended to help set this up.
Some Tax Forms You'll Need	Form 1120 – Corporate Income Tax Return. Form 1120 W – Estimated Corporate Tax Payroll Tax, State and local business and sales tax, etc.
Type	**Corporation – S Corp**
Definition	Same as C Corp. This is more popular than the C Corp. The main difference is that with the S Corp, profits and losses are reflected on your own 1040 returns as opposed to on the corporation's.
Pluses	Same as C Corp. Profits from S corporation are passed through to shareholders based on their shares owned. Losses are passed through to shareholders based on their shares owned but only to their capital investment and personal loans made to the

corporation. No corporate income taxes are due on S Corps.

Minuses	Same as C Corporation
Some Tax Forms You'll Need	Form 1120 – S Corporate Income Tax Return.
	1120 S K1
	Payroll Tax, State and local business and sales tax, etc.

Type	**Limited Liability Corporation (LLC)**
Definition	This is becoming a very popular arrangement for small businesses as it combines the elements of a corporation with the tax benefits and relative ease of use of a partnership.
Pluses	Flexible and less formal than a traditional corporation.
Minuses	Can get expensive and there's more paperwork to fill out to get started.
Some Tax Forms You'll Need	Legally, a single person can form an LLC. If you have a partner, you'll need the same forms as a partnership. All income and Social Security taxes are paid on partners' tax returns, form 1040, 1040SE; State and local business and sales tax, etc.

Not all businesses require licenses (for instance, you don't need a catering license in the state of North Carolina) but you'll need to find out what licenses and forms your state requires. Look under the City Business License Office in the phone book. Also, the Small Business Assistance Center (www.sbacnetwork.org) provides free counseling, seminars and financial referrals for small business owners. If you want to incorporate, check out a company called My Corporation (www.mycorporation.com). You'll pay for the service but you'll save a lot of paperwork and headache.

Taxes

If you're sloppy with your checkbook, you'd better whip yourself into shape fast. You won't be able to get away with this in your business. Whether it's monthly projected earnings you'll be reporting or sending in timely sales tax, you'll have to be more organized than ever before so the IRS doesn't come a-knockin'. Hiring a part-time accountant'll help ease the stress of doing it right the first time. Before you sell one muffin, you'll have to have all of your documents in place. These include an *Employer Identification Number* from the federal government as well as *State Tax Information*. The Federal Department of Revenue is the place to apply for these documents (www.irs.gov). Click on businesses and then small business for a list of what you'll need. The IRS also offers free virtual workshops where you can learn about everything from payroll taxes to electronic filing. Remember: you'll need to file both federal and state taxes.

Trademarks, Patents and Copyrights

A *trademark*™ or *service mark*℠ is a word or symbol associated with a particular entity. The trademark will serve to identify your product or service as well as be used to market that business. A business name is something that would be trademarked, in addition to a tag line such as Nike® *Just Do It*. If you have a catchy name for your business, you'll likely want to register it with the Trademark Office so that once you start marketing your product, you'll be protected for a period of ten years. To clear up a common confusion: anyone can use the ™ sign as a way of claiming rights to a particular mark, regardless of whether that mark is filed with the United States Patent and Trademark Office. An ® can only be used, however, *after* the USPTO grants a trademark in connection with a particular good or service but offers more legal protection than a ™. Be prepared to shell out a few hundred dollars for your mark (the basic filing fee is $335). Also, applying for a trademark takes several months time, so keep this in mind when working on your business plan and marketing campaign.

A *patent* is a legal document issued to an inventor by the U.S. Patent and Trademark Office for a period of time (usually twenty years). A patent protects the inventor by excluding others from making or selling the same invention during that time. This one will cost you the most, as you'll probably want to consult an attorney. On your own, you'll incur filing fees upwards of $700. For more information on patents and trademarks, or to file for either electronically, log on to the United States Patent and Trademark Office (www.uspto.gov).

A *copyright* is used to protect intellectual property, such as a book, music or screenplay. The work must be completed before you can copyright it. A copyright is relatively easy and inexpensive to obtain (fees are $30). You can do this by submitting a copy of the finished work along with payment and information to the United States Copyright Office. To do this electronically, log on to www.copyright.gov.

Free Money

Financing your business is the most difficult piece of the pie. Before you think about loans, I suggest doing a little research to see if you can get some free money in the form of a grant. There are plenty of organizations out there looking to give away their money to good businesses—particularly not-for-profits and minority owned. The best place to start your research is at the Foundation Center (www.fdncenter.org). Foundation libraries can be found in major cities such as New York, Atlanta, San Francisco and Washington, D.C. Here, you can spend hours (or days) sifting through binders of material on grant bestowing organizations. You can also sign up for seminars on how to begin looking for a grant to help you narrow down your search. The process is worthwhile, even if you're not even thinking about a grant right now. The librarians are chock full of information, so bring a bag lunch and spend the day asking a lot of questions. If you can't get to a Foundation Library, you can also log on to the Small Business Administration website (www.sba.gov). Make sure you check out the area specifically targeting women-owned businesses, and click on Grant Resources in the Financing Your Business section.

Loans

If you come up dry from the free money sources, you'll probably have to consider a small business loan. A potential lender will want to know that you're serious about your business. This means you need to be organized and have all of your paperwork in order when you apply for your loan. The business plan will come in handy. Chances are, you'll be asking about a *Short Term Loan*, which will need to be paid back within a relatively short period of time (usually within a year). One word of caution: Be sure your personal financial situation is in good standing. Do you have good credit? Do you have any collateral (something tangible that can serve as a backup) for your loan? Many times, a lender will look at this first, even if your business plan is perfectly crafted. Why? Because even a perfectly crafted business can fail. If you're a homeowner, you may be in a better position to get a loan than a renter, but each lending institution differs, so make sure to compare your options carefully.

The Small Business Administration offers loan programs, so check their website for detailed information on how to apply. You may also qualify for a non-profit loan or a physical disaster business loan, depending on the nature of your business and where you're located.

There are lots of different loan options available to you if you do the research. You can find loads of information at the Office of Women's Business Ownership (www.onlinewbc.gov) for resources in your area.

Creative Ways of Finding Space

Finding the right space to set up shop can be incredibly frustrating to a small business owner. Karen W. was all set to open her delivery food business out of her apartment in Atlanta. When she went to apply for her business license, she was all but laughed out of the office because her company wasn't located in a commercial catering kitchen. The health inspector wouldn't even consider her business until this was done. Lesson here? Be sure to know your business and its limitations.

Obviously a food-related business will require more scrutiny, but you can be creative here too. Some of the best resources may be right in your own neighborhood. Churches, synagogues, community centers and not-for-profits are all good choices if you're thinking of opening a catering business or the likes. Many have certified commercial kitchens and only use them for dinners and an occasional meeting here and there. You'll save a load of cash by renting from them. You can probably work out a deal with the organization that benefits you both. Your local Chamber of Commerce, Visitor and Convention Center's Bureau or City Council Office can help you get started. You'll also need to contact your state's Planning and Zoning office to make sure you're permitted to operate your business from the location you choose.

Business Insurance

A good business insurance policy can mean the difference between your company's success and failure. Hopefully, you'll never have to use it. Too many small business start-ups overlook this essential piece, thinking "Oh, it's just myself and a partner; what could go wrong?" Well, anything. The last thing you need is a lawsuit on your shoulders should someone decide they were wronged by your enterprise. If you're serving food, it's absolutely imperative that you get insurance, in case someone gets sick from your lemon meringue. If you'll be using your car to deliver your goods (or hiring delivery people), you'll need to get extra coverage for that too.

In addition to *General Liability Coverage*, which serves as the starting point for most business insurance policies, you'll add on extras depending on the nature of your business. Shop around for the best policy out there. This is time consuming, especially since you'll be considered "high risk" if you've never worked in your line of business before. Take a look at www.netquote.com to get started.

Charging a Fair Price

After assessing the marketplace, you'll need to come up with a fair price to charge your customers. Discover what others charge for the same product or service. How different is your product from the competition? How much more will someone pay for it (keeping taxes, salaries, any extra fees into consideration)? Obviously the idea is to turn a profit. When you set a price, you want to base this on what you'll *net*. This is money you get after all the expenses are taken out. A good way to remember this is to think of money falling through an actual net. What's left in the net is what you keep! Remember you're going to spend a lot more in the beginning for start-up costs.

Hiring Employees

If you plan on hiring employees and having them work full-time, you'll need to offer benefits compensation and deal with payroll tax. This can be overwhelming to first time small business owners, but it's something you should think about for the future. You'll also need to pay employment taxes. Make sure to read up on employee compensation on the IRS website (www.irs.gov). Something else to remember as a general rule: if you're good to your employees, they'll be good to you. Creating a pleasant work environment and listening to the needs of your workers (without being a pushover) will pay off in the long term. If you've never managed people before, this can be a real challenge. The more people you hire, the more personalities you'll encounter. A good suggestion is to sign up for a seminar on small business management offered by a human resources specialist. You'll learn a lot about yourself as well as your own management style.

Marketing, Marketing, Marketing

No matter how great you imagine your business will be, if you don't know how to market it, you might as well not open. Some of the most absurd ideas are huge successes, while brilliant ones are left in the dust. Why? Marketing. It's more important than the product itself.

This can be a daunting process if you aren't organized. Successful marketing involves knowing your business inside-out as well as understanding the demographic you're targeting. To keep yourself from getting overwhelmed, keep a file of marketing ideas as soon as you begin thinking about your business itself. Spend half your day working on your business and the other half thinking about marketing it. Marketing can get very costly, so you'll need to have an idea of what you're willing to spend. Here are some basics to help launch your campaign:

• **Branding** – This is a process which associates a name, tag line, or image with a particular product or service. Advertising execs throw around this term around left and right. The idea is to take your business, assign a name and / or logo to it and get the word out like mad. You want the name and logo to be consistent with everything that's connected with your business. From letterhead to delivery bags, books to a line of dolls, a consistent look and feel to your business' name and design will help brand it in the marketplace. As much as I hate to use the example, think Olsen Twins. They've got a marketing genius behind them. Some ways to help you brand your business include the following:

• **Securing a Domain Name** – When thinking of domain names, try to use something that'll be easy for people to remember if they're doing a search online. Everyone gobbled up the dot coms in the early 90s but now there's plenty of choices to go around, even if it's a dot.net, dot.tv, or dot.us. In terms of your name, getting too abstract will make it difficult for people to find your product or service (unless you're a marketing goddess and can brand the heck out of some random title that doesn't mean anything). Again, be realistic about how you're going to market your product so you don't wind up with a half-baked campaign.

Once you have a name in mind, log on to www.register.com to check if your domain name has been taken. When you find one that's available, you can buy it for about $30 a year. Hire a web designer (or do it yourself) to put together a site for you. One page may be all you need depending on your business. If you're selling your product online, it'll cost more to have a secure shopping cart system set up. You can also do this through PayPal (www.paypal.com). No matter what you're doing, people will check you out online, so you really need some sort of web presence.

When you have your domain name secured and your website ready, you'll want to make sure you get top visibility. You can do this by submitting your website to search engines such as Google and Yahoo (for a fee), but you may not necessarily be the first page pulled up when people do a search for a product or service. Web marketing is a whole world of its own and warrants more research. I suggest reading *World Wide Web Marketing: Integrating the Web into Your Marketing Strategy* by Jim Sterne, John, Wiley & Sons.

• **Trade Shows** – Whatever your business, there are at least ten trade shows that cater to it. We talked about being a presenter in Chapter Three: *So You Wanna Be a Doorman*, but now, if you're serious about your business, you should attend a few of these as an exhibitor. It's a great place to check out the competition as well as get some marketing ideas—not to mention meet potential customers and network. From gift shows to cooking expos to book fairs to college activities, there's a show for your company somewhere out there. Do a Google search under "trade shows" in your area of business. A good way to save money is to attend a regional show rather than a national show. You'll save on the booth fees and can still make some great contacts. Make sure you have ample brochures, business cards and any other literature on hand to give out when people stop by. Since this stuff can get costly, try and find a graphic design student to help you out. Not only will you get very creative stuff, they may even be able to help you find a printer for less.

• **Mailing Lists** – Pre-packaged mailing labels are the way to go for direct mail campaigns. Here, you specify what types of people you're looking to target (lists can be sorted by zip code, household income, or interest, as well as in lots of other ways). You'll pay for a set of labels, which'll be mailed to you. There are too many companies to mention offering all kinds of label services combined with direct mail packages. Surf around and see what suits your needs.

• **Postcards** – Self-mailers or postcards are a good way to launch your direct mail marketing campaign. Try Modern Postcard (www.modernpostcard.com) for fast turnaround at very reasonable prices.

• **Help!** – Consider hiring a college student to help you market your product or service. You'd be surprised how resourceful they are (remember, you were once there!) You can even offer an unpaid (or low paid) internship through area colleges and universities—even high schools. Interns are great for data entry, phone calls, mailings and other time-consuming tasks, not to mention coffee. I know this because I was one . . . frequently. But *please* be nice to your interns.

And the Number One Free Marketing Resource is . . . .

• **Word of Mouth!** – Remember the "turn one person into five" rule from Chapter Four: *Opening the Door*? Well, try turning one person into 5,000. Spread the good word and your business will take off. I don't care if you have to hire people to do it (hey, it worked for the Beatles). Get your friends to go nuts telling people about your business. Offer free samples, stand on street corners, call your old ballet instructor, organize free seminars, book readings and theatrical showcases at your local library, pull out all the stops! If you don't have money to spend on a huge marketing campaign, you're going to have to use your mouth. Talk it up, baby.

Additional Business Resources for Entrepreneurs

National Organizations

Catalyst Women: www.catalystwomen.org – Provides a wealth of information and research tools on and for women in business.

National Association of Women Business Owners: www.nawbo.org – Represents the interests of women business owners around the country. Also, a source for contacts and networking.

Small Business Administration: www.sba.gov – Mentioned before but I'll list here too.

www.Onlinewbc.gov – Part of the Small Business Administration, here you can find a comprehensive listing of other women's business organizations that may offer networking events in your area.

www.entrepreneur.com – An online community and print magazine.

Chicago

www.wehaveanswers.org – Offers resources for entrepreneurs and small business owners; free consulting and workshops in Chicago.

Los Angeles

www.worksourcecalifornia.com – Operated by the Workforce Investment Board, they can supply employees for your business in California.

www.lacity.org/cdd – The City of Los Angeles Community Development Department offers many different business services for small entrepreneurs to large commercial developers.

New York

http://www2.nypl.org/smallbiz/ – Offers local resources and small business assistance for entrepreneurs in the New York area.

Chapter 6
Take it to the Couch
Some words on mental health

If you're like most women, you've probably thought about therapy at some point in your life. After processing the information from the previous chapters, you're probably thinking about it even more. And if you're planning on living in a place like New York City, chances are you'll actually be in therapy in the next few months. It seems as if city people all have shrinks and they like to talk about them. To quote Jerry Seinfeld, "Not that there's anything wrong with that." Even if you're super motivated and can get over most things with a good run and the sound track to *Grease*, sometimes you just need some extra help. That's where therapy comes in.

Therapy was once taboo and only something people did when they had a "serious problem." Today it's so common and diverse, you could go nuts (pardon the pun) trying to figure out the various types. The good thing is—thanks to people like Tipper Gore—the word "therapy" is wide out in the open. Just walk down the street and you'll hear someone talking about her shrink.

What's important to know before anyone starts playing with your head, however, is that there are different methods to therapy. I think they're more like religions. People who practice different types of therapy believe so wholeheartedly in their type that you could get brainwashed if you're not careful. And then you're really going to need therapy.

In all seriousness, therapy is not something that should be taken lightly. It's time consuming, it's expensive (unless you can get your insurance to pay for it) and it's hard work. Just sitting in there like a lump isn't going to make you better either. Therapy doesn't work by osmosis.

So, how do you know if therapy's right for you? Well, aside from the fact that most therapists will say everyone can use a little, some situations are more urgent in nature and require immediate attention. Ask yourself the following questions:

- Do I have trouble making a decision?
- Do I cry a lot for no apparent reason?

- Do I feel fulfilled in my relationships?
- Is my mood erratic and unpredictable?
- Do I obsess over the little things on a regular basis?
- Do I need other people's approval for everything I do?
- Am I an obsessive drinker, drug user, eater, shopper, smoker, sex-aholic, gambler, etc.?
- Do I constantly find myself in situations that I can't get out of?
- Do I feel the need to please others more than I do myself?
- Do I feel stuck in a troubled relationship, career or other life situation?
- Am I too competitive with myself?
- Am I able to interact with people?
- Do I have trouble sleeping or concentrating?
- Am I intensely paranoid to the point where it interferes with my relationships?
- Do I like myself?
- Do I worry too much?
- Am I happy?

Now, after beating yourself up over these questions, take a deep breath. You probably are surprised at how many you answered "Yes" to. Yeah, me too. Whether you answered yes to one or ten of the above questions, it's important to know about the different types of therapy out there. The last thing you want to do is hook yourself up with a quack. No matter which type you choose, make sure you research the therapist personally. Try to get referrals. You should also know there are a tremendous number of support groups on all sorts of mental health issues—from sleep disorders to alcoholism—should you want to be with other people who are dealing with a similar issue. In terms of one-on-one help, here's a quick look at some of the most common types of therapies practiced today:

Cognitive (Cognitive-Behavioral)

Cognitive therapy has become increasingly popular among young people in recent years. Its practice focuses on the present rather than the past. Based on a more realistic approach to thinking, cognitive therapy teaches short-term problem-solving skills that can be applied to specific life situations. As a result, you change the way in which you perceive, and ultimately respond to, those situations. Don't be surprised if you're given homework to do between sessions, which can help speed up your progress. While not a quick fix by any means, treatment may only require a few sessions.

Best candidates for Cognitive Therapy:

- Those who're goal oriented.
- Those who want to take a hands-on approach to solving their problems.
- Those who may only be affected by one particular disorder such as fears, eating disorders, substance abuse or obsessions. More recently however, cognitive therapy has also been shown to be effective for co-occurring disorders.

To find a cognitive therapist near you, log on to the Academy of Cognitive Therapy website (www.academyofct.org). They have a low cost therapist referral program that you can access by typing in your zip code.

For additional information on Cognitive / Behavioral Therapy log on to:

www.beckinstitute.org

www.aabt.org

In New York: www.cognitivetherapynyc.com

Psychotherapy / Psychoanalysis

Based on Sigmund Freud's belief that all behavior stems from unconscious motivation, psychotherapy is a treatment to understand conflict and problems, with the goal being personality growth, self-awareness and behavioral change. Treatment can range anywhere from a few months to many years, depending upon the patient. The therapy often digs deep into childhood and adolescent events and feelings, even those that the patient may not consciously remember, to understand current problems.

For those who really want to get into it, you may be a candidate for *Psychoanalysis*. This is where you get down and dirty and lie on the couch. Psychoanalysts have gone through extensive training as well as years of their own concentrated therapy. The process is a very intensive (and intense) process that can last years. It requires an incredible commitment from the patient. But, for those who have gone through it, many swear by it. They believe it's changed their lives.

Best candidates for Psychoanalysis:

- Those who're willing to dedicate a lot of time and energy to getting to the root of the problem and who're in touch with their inner self.

- Those who can talk freely about family and intimate relationships.
- Those who can't quite figure out what's wrong.
- Those who associate sex with everything.

Additional information on certain types of psychotherapy and psychoanalysis can be found by contacting the New York Freudian Society Referral Service at 212.873.7029 or by logging on to www.nyfreudian.org.

Psychiatry vs. Psychology

A *psychiatrist* is a medical doctor, licensed to treat patients as well as administer medication for mental illness. He or she has gone through four years of medical school plus an additional four plus years of clinical experience. A clinical psychologist may hold a Sc.D. or a Ph.D., but not an M.D. While both psychiatrists and psychologists are trained in the areas of therapy and mental illness and have gone through a tremendous amount of schooling, the main difference between the two is that psychologists cannot prescribe medication.

You've probably heard a lot about drugs such as Prozac, Paxil and Zoloft, in addition to a newer drug now on the market, Lexapro. These are the ones most commonly used to treat depression. Categorized as Seratonin Specific Reuptake Inhibitors (SSRI drugs), they increase the amount of seratonin (a neurotransmitter) in the brain, which improves your mood. These drugs are marketed to help people with generalized anxiety disorders, sleep disorders, depression, stress, panic attacks or obsessive-compulsive disorders. The side effects vary from drug to drug and range from decreased libido to weight gain, increased heart rate to insomnia and dry mouth. If you feel you need medication to deal with your issues, it's highly recommended that you see a psychiatrist. In addition, any reputable psychologist or other type of therapist will refer you to the appropriate clinician or pscychopharmacologist should he or she feel medication is necessary.

For more information on psychiatry contact the American Psychiatric Association at www.psych.org.

Best candidates for Psychiatry:

- Those who want a more conventional approach to mental health from a medical perspective.

• Those who feel they need drugs to treat a problem.

Best candidates for Psychology:

> • Treatment varies depending on the type of psychology practiced by a therapist. Consult the American Psychological Association's website at www.apa.org for a comprehensive listing of therapies.

Social Worker

A licensed social worker has a minimum of two years of social work school plus additional work experience in a professional setting. Some may have more experience in clinical settings, hospitals, managed care facilities, schools or non-profit organizations. While many social workers also function as therapists, it's up to you to decide if the therapy they provide is adequate. Many social workers are hired by organizations to help clients with practical issues such as job hunting, housing and filing legal papers. Often by default, however, they act more as therapists and may even see private patients. Social workers' fees typically aren't as astronomical as a psychotherapist's (a trained psychotherapist in NYC can get up to $300 per hour, and just so you know, many have social work degrees) but then again, they also haven't been through as much training. You may find that a social worker is helpful depending on your situation and its magnitude.

Best candidates for social work:

> • Those who may need counseling for practical issues relating to legal, job, financial, family or housing matters.
>
> • Those who're dealing with terminal illness, emotional problems or substance abuse and are part of a program in a hospital or other institution. Families of these individuals may also benefit from the social worker's services as well.
>
> • Those who have access to a social worker on-staff at their place of business and find their services adequate to help them work through a difficult period in their lives.

To find a social worker near you, contact the National Association of Social Workers at www.socialworkers.org.

Holistic Therapy

Holistic therapy looks at the individual as a whole in relation to her surroundings. Areas of particular focus are the senses: sight, smell, sound and touch. Often combined with alternative treatments such as acupuncture, acupressure, aromatherapy or herbal remedies, holistic therapy may also employ music, dance, art or animals (it's not what you're thinking) as part of the treatment process. While unconventional in nature, holistic therapy is becoming increasingly popular. For those who choose this route, it's important to note that holistic therapy is not supported by many medical professionals. This doesn't mean it can't work for you, but as with all therapy, you should be extra cautious when choosing your therapist. Be wary of those who promise miracles or make unrealistic claims. Find out if your therapist is known in your community, or if he has written any papers for scientific journals. Do your research. A great place to start is with the National Institute of Health. Log on to:

www.nlm.nih.gov/medlineplus/alternativemedicine.html

Best candidates for Holistic Therapy:

- Those who are looking for an unconventional approach to treating their problems.
- Those who've had success with acupuncture or acupressure or other similar treatments.

Art Therapy / Dance Therapy / Music Therapy

I grouped these together because they all basically have the same philosophy behind them: Use your creative inner self to figure out what is wrong with you. And, you can kill two birds with one stone here: Fix your head; take an art class. I'm not joking. By listening to music, drawing a picture or participating in some sort of creative expression, the therapist uses art to connect with the patient's emotions.

You'll find many music, art and dance therapists employed in hospitals working with children where the only way to communicate is using creative expression. But it's known to work well for adults too. So, if you're interested in learning more, check out these organizations: www.arttherapy.org or www.musictherapy.org

Best candidates for Art, Music or Dance therapy:

- Those who are seeking creative approaches to mental health.
- Those who are part of a program employing art, dance or music as part of their treatment.

Clergy

Sometimes a good dose of the cloth is all you need. If you're going through a specific period of difficulty (such as divorce, death in the family, relationship woes, etc.) and feel a connection to a particular religious institution, you may want to talk with your priest or rabbi. Clergy are trained in social services as well as theology. And, best of all, it won't cost you a dime.

Best candidates for clergy:

- Those who are figuring out where to turn for help. Clergy is sometimes a good first stop.
- Those who can't afford to pay for any type of traditional therapy.
- Those who're involved in their church, temple or synagogue and feel comfortable in a religious setting.

Interviewing a Therapist

It was hard enough going to the first session—now what happens if you don't like your choice? Well, you'll have to shop around, just like with anything else. It can get a little tricky, but you need to feel confident with your therapist before you start the hard work.

Some therapists are like gyms. You get locked into so many sessions that nothing short of your own death can get you out of it. But, since this is probably something you want to avoid (which is why you came to therapy in the first place), you're going to have to decide if your therapy is working for you and *then* decide to stick with it or not. Don't mistake hard work for not liking your therapist. There'll be days when you absolutely hate her—but this doesn't mean it's not working. Only you will be able to judge the effectiveness of the treatment, so be honest with yourself. If you truly feel the therapy isn't making you think a little differently about yourself at all by the fifth or sixth session, you may want to consider trying someone else. Just be prepared to be firm with your therapist so you don't spend your hour analyzing why you're choosing to go elsewhere.

When you do go to your first session, here are some questions you may want to ask:

- Where did you do your training?
- How does your type of therapy work?
- When will I notice changes in myself?
- Do you offer a payment plan (sometimes called a sliding scale)?

 • Do you have any references?

Paying for Therapy

Will my work know?

Most health insurance plans have a mental health division, which can refer you to a host of mental health clinicians. But they'll only send you a list, not a personal recommendation. If you go through your employer's insurance, the human resources department will know you're getting therapy. If you don't want your employer to know this, you may opt to bypass reporting your treatment to your insurance. But, this also means that you will have to pay out of pocket—and that can get costly. Average fees for therapists range from $50 to well over $250 an hour, depending on your city and specialist. One thing you should always do up-front is ask your therapist about payment plans. Many will work with you if you're on a tight budget and reduce their fees to accommodate your needs. This may be especially true for a budding therapist fresh out of training. Many are eager to start a practice and you'd be surprised how skilled they are.

General Therapy Resources

Any college or university in your area will have resources on affordable mental health providers in your area. You may not be able to visit an on-campus clinic if you're not affiliated with the institution, but it's always worth a call to find out for sure.

Also, you'll get a lot of information at The Anxiety Disorders Association of America (www.adaa.org).

City Specific Therapy Resources

Chicago

Access Community Health Network
www.accesscommunityhealth.net
866.882.2237
Over forty health center organizations throughout Chicago providing health care regardless of your ability to pay.
The Medical Group
773.978.5700
Confidential services for women, including counseling, public aid and student discounts available.

Los Angeles

The Los Angeles Free Clinic
www.lafreeclinic.org
With locations all over L.A., this clinic offers a wide range of health care services and resources.

New York

Center for Educational and Psychological Services
Teachers College, Columbia University
www.tc.edu/ceps
212.678.3262
Fees range from $5-$40. You'll see graduate students trained in all areas of therapy.
National Institute for the Psychotherapies (NIP)
www.nipinst.org
212.582.1566
Offers reduced fees for students and those who are unemployed with proof of financial status.

San Francisco

Therapy Network

www.therapynetwork.net

415.974.9779

A not-for-profit organization offering referrals for psychotherapists.

Chapter 7
Dating Yourself
A solo gal's guide to the leisure life

We've all been there: Mateless. It's especially annoying when your girlfriends are planning their weddings and you're supposed to be happy for them. But all you can think about is the fact that you're going to be thirty (okay, so maybe its in five years) and you don't even have a boyfriend. That means you've got a year to find one, a year of courtship, a year of planning the wedding and, assuming you didn't have a shotgun, you'll want at least two years to be with the guy before you have kids. Which makes you, like, fifty before you're going to have a baby—and that's too old!

Deep breath. It's okay. More women are having kids later in life these days. Look at Madonna!

First of all, it's not that bad. Second of all, there's more to life than meeting someone. I mean, look at the divorce rate—to the moon. And if you ask me, there's only one reason for it: people aren't happy with themselves. Like many of our parents, nobody had time to figure it out before they met their mate. So, look at it as a chance to change the stats. Laugh at your friends who got married at twenty-one. They're all going to get divorced anyway. Just kidding. Go out on your own now so you don't have to do it later. And that brings me to dating yourself.

Dating yourself is actually pretty fun. You can basically pick anything you want to do and don't have to deal with some-one else's opinion about how to do it. Think movies, shows, museums and restaurants—even trips if you're daring. The first time I went to a restaurant alone (okay, the first few times), I put a book by the other seat to make it look like someone was joining me. But I got over it. Now, I walk in with confidence, not caring what the hostess thinks. I order wine, appetizers, a full entrée—even dessert. Yep. I go to a movie, I get a large tub of popcorn; I eat it by myself. Now that I'm married (yes, I did finally get married), I still go out alone. But I spent many a year dating myself. It's *fun*. Really. You're not a loser if you go out by yourself. You're *cool!* And, you're more likely to get a ticket to a hot concert or Broadway show as a single rather than a couple. I still do it today. But just so you don't even have to put any more thought into this than you want to, here are some suggestions for some great solo dates, all affordably priced (hey, who's picking up the tab here?), of course.

The Equestrian

Start with a hearty breakfast at the local diner. Go for the gusto: eggs, bacon, grits (if you live down South), toast and a glass of juice. Wait half an hour—swimming rules apply—and then head down to the stables for a riding lesson. There're no excuses for you city folk either. See the list at the end of the chapter for suggestions.

The Poet

Literature and latte—my two favorite combinations. Since you can't take coffee into the library, why not spend the evening at your favorite bookstore? Not only is this a fun place to people watch, but it's free (well, not the latte)! Whether you want to search for a classic novel, read up on a hobby or scan every magazine on the racks for a new haircut, you'll lose track of time and have a pleasant solo evening. There's just something about bookstores at night. In Los Angeles, try Book Soup or Skylight Books. In Chicago there's Barbara's Books; in San Francisco the Booksmith; in Denver The Tattered Cover; in Washington, D.C. Olsson's Books; and in New York, Shakespeare & Co., just to name a few. Lots of public libraries offer free book clubs too. Check 'em out in Chicago, Denver and Seattle.

The Tiger

Nothing like a little driving range to get your juices flowing. I love hitting a golf ball (that is, when I can hit it). It's clean, it's fun and it's really cheap. You can find a driving range in 'most any city. Buckets of balls generally range from $4 to $20 depending on where you live.

The Scavenger

Antiquing, renovating, stripping (furniture, that is) or discount *tchotchke* shopping, even if you've got money to spare, this *goin' solo* gal's always looking for a deal. Your date begins by seeking out flea markets, antique shops or garage sales in the Friday paper and spending your Saturday searching for finds. It's amazing what you can do with a piece of sandpaper and some polyurethane. In addition to the flea markets listed in Chapter

One: *Keeping House*, you'll find some fun day trips near major cities listed at the end of the chapter.

The Animal Lover

Adopt a pet—for the weekend. Before you can even utter "But I don't have the money," consider adopting a Seeing Eye Dog™ in training. All you have to do is prove you're normal, then provide shelter and food for two days. No hassles, no commitment. Call your local Humane Society to find out if this program is offered near you.

The Bounty Hunter

This is a fun activity, even if you haven't just broken up with someone. Not that I recommend this on a weekly basis, but every now and then, a firing range is just what a *goin' solo* gal needs (and no, I'm not a card carrying member of the NRA). If you don't like guns, you can also try going to an archery range. Personally, it's not as gratifying, but at least you can practice your aim. Check the listings at the end of the chapter for locations.

The Food Connoisseur

Cooking classes are a great way to explore your own creativity, meet some new people and enjoy delicious food. You can find these offered at many local colleges or universities under their Continuing Education Programs, as well as in fine restaurants or culinary institutes. And you don't have to spend a lot of money either. You'll find some inexpensive city options listed at the end of the chapter.

The Race Car Driver

Admit it, you've always wanted to drive a stick shift but you don't know how. Well, now's your chance to learn. You sat there at the arcade playing *Turbo* just so you could move that stupid thing around, didn't you? I did, and, uh, it didn't exactly work. But after crashing two of my friend's cars, I finally learned. And let me tell you something: not only is driving a stick one hundred times more fun than driving an automatic, but you'll feel empowered beyond your wildest dreams. Find someone to lend you her car (don't borrow the BMW), or rent a wreck (www.rentawreck.com) for the weekend and learn.

The Shopper

Did you think I'd leave this one out? Nothing helps to pass the time more than getting a great deal on a hot outfit. From sample sales to funky boutiques, spend an evening in the dressing room, even if you're just going home afterwards and changing back into your P.J.s. You'll find great deals at the stores listed at the end of the chapter.

Solo Party Hosting

For those of you who absolutely cannot go out alone, there are other ways to have a good time. One of them is to throw a party for no reason at all. Yes, yes—the thought of hosting people alone for any type of event *is* frightening. And with limited budgets and never enough time, making pine cone topiaries on a Tuesday afternoon is ridiculous, let alone pretty. Sorry, Martha. But just because you work hard and live alone doesn't mean you can't be the belle of your own ball. Throwing a party solo can be loads of fun. It's a chance to say "I don't need a mate to have an event." And it'll give you something to look forward to—believe me, we all need that. In terms of reasons to have a party, do you really need one? No, but it's always fun. Here are some ideas for you to try:

Party Theme Ideas

• **Singles Mixer –** Have each of your friends bring someone who's single. Don't try to mix and match here—just let the evening unfold on its own.

What to serve: Hey, you're mixing and matching guests, why not mix and match food? Try the nacho cheese dip and stir fry up some frozen veggie dumplings. Serve with a pitcher with sangria. Or, have everyone bring one person and one dish—just make sure they don't all bring the same dish (or the same person).

• **Tea Party –** This is a really nice afternoon party for the ladies. You can make a variety of teas and serve with milk, honey or caramel. Be creative with sandwiches and desserts. Ask your guests to wear funky hats.

What to serve: Cucumber, Alouette cheese spread on white bread, cut up in triangles (no crusts, please), pretzels in honey mustard sauce, party ryes with lox spread. Anything dainty works, just make a lot so you don't starve!

• **Murder Mystery Party –** A fun alternative to typical New Year's Eve mayhem. There are a few board games out there that orchestrate an entire murder mystery evening. Find some great ones on www.areyougame.com. Buy the game beforehand and tell your guests to dress the part. Dinner can also be part of the theme.

What to serve: A murder in a Tuscan villa calls for pasta and lots of red wine, while a mystery on the Nile can be combined with a Middle Eastern fest of hummus, salads, pita and chicken kabobs. Don't be afraid to get a little wacky. Then again, you can always just order Chinese.

• **P.J. Party with Masseuse** – Everybody loves getting a massage. Stop by your local nail salon and find out how much they would charge to send a masseuse up to your place for a few hours of manicures and massages for your gal pals. For some reason this is really cheap in cities like New York and Los Angeles, perhaps due to the overwhelming number of nail salons. It's also a fun way to host a bridal shower, birthday party or end a really stressful week at work.

What to Serve: Anything on a stick so you don't mess up your nails.

• **Remodeling Party★** – Like the show *Trading Spaces*? Why not create your own version? Maybe you've always wanted to redecorate, but just don't have the "touch." Invite your friends for an assessment and demolition party, get rid of the junk and figure out what you can salvage. Paint, stencil and sand away. Give each friend a job and let them each use their talents to make your pad a little more spiffy.

★Note: this party is not a good idea if you're a control freak.

What to serve: Trade recipes. Have each of your friends bring a dish and the recipe that goes along with it.

• **I-Hate-the-Superbowl-But-Love-the-Food Party** – This is where you put the Superbowl on low so it *looks* like you're watching, but truly the only reason you're getting everyone together is so that you can eat chips, dips and pigs in blankets with a purpose. For those who want to actually watch, have a TV set up in another room, but keep the real partying focused around the food.

What to serve: Velveeta dip, pigs-in-blankets, potato skins, baked Brie, beer. Anything fattening and cheap.

And just to get a little more imaginative, here are some other ideas for solo hosted parties.

• **I-Got-Rejected party!** (Can also be done as an I-Got-Fired Party, I-Got-Laid-Off Party, I-Got-Laid-Off-*Again* party, I-Got-Dumped Party, etc.) – This is where you say "the heck with it" to convention and lack of money. Just go ahead and indulge! Have everything you've ever wanted but couldn't eat because of Atkins on one plate: peanut butter cups, ice cream and hot fudge, high fat potato chips, real sour cream and onion dip and double cheese pizza. Don't forget lots of wine and maybe even a few Jello shots for old times sake.

There's no organization to this party—just sheer madness. Invite your friends over and allow your cute little apartment to become a total dump. Take out your aggressions on the food, the alcohol, the guy your friend brought—just make sure you've got people to help you clean up the next day. Your true friends will stay. When the eating's done, have some down pillows on hand for an all-out pillow fight—one final stage of aggression. Make sure the feathers go everywhere, even in the dip. The place should look like a sty when you're done. If you're really nervous, hide the important stuff and cover the floor with garbage bags first. This is what I did—uh, I mean what I *would* do.

• **I'm-Not-Cool-Enough-for-"Sex and the City" Party** – This is where you and your friends wear the sexiest possible outfit you can find in your own closet and then see how it matches up (or doesn't) to the gals from *Sex and the City*. Make your own cocktails and pretend you can actually get into a place like *Pangea*. Then compare cellulite and eat some more chips.

Some of the best parties are simply the ones thrown together at the last minute. Don't feel as if you have to have everyone under the sun either. Small, intimate groups where everyone contributes something are always nice. When you're working, it's always the last minute stuff that takes the most time. Have each friend bring something easy, but something that you don't need to deal with: a loaf of bread, olives, salsa and chips, dessert. Give people categories and you'll cover your bases. Often times I'll take care of the main course and have my pals bring the rest. They still feel as if they're being entertained, but I don't have to worry about accessorizing with side dishes. The recipes at the end of the chapter can help you out.

Décor

You don't need to go crazy with decorations, but it'll help to have some sort of creative stuff around the place if you're throwing a bash.

• **Centerpieces** – Don't spend money on these. Having a fall party? Throw a pumpkin in the middle of the table and grab some leaves off your street (or the park) and sprinkle around.

- **Christmas or Holiday party?** – Buy a $3 bag of red and green confetti, or sprinkle some Hanukkah Gelt around the table for a festive look. I highly recommend taking full advantage of the 99 Cent Store if there's one near you. They've got candles galore, which always make a place look festive.
- **Summer Bash?** – Buy a few blow-up beach balls at the drug store and toss them around your apartment. You can also buy a few packs of children's sunglasses and put them on your serving trays with summer fruits to garnish.
- **Party favors?** – Fuhgeddaboudit.

Alcohol

This is where so many parties get costly. Some advice: ask your guests to bring the booze. Hey, you're taking care of the food and venue; they can throw in a bottle of wine, for cryin' out loud. Ten guests, seven bottles (assume some people will forget). But, if you just have to do it all yourself, the answer is: *buy in bulk*. So what if it's cheap wine? Just throw some orange and apple slices in with it and make Sangria. That way it'll mask the taste of the cheapness. Costco, Sam's Club, BJ's—they've got it all. See what I'm talking about? You don't need a $20 bottle of Chardonnay—get the $7 bottle and throw some seltzer and a lime in it. Can you spell s-p-r-i-t-z-e-r? Let one of your friends be on mixer duty. This'll keep you free to meet and greet your guests.

Another idea is to bag the bar altogether and go with a punch bowl. This way, you can jazz up even the cheapest alcohol with some fruit, HI C and a decorative ice ring (see recipe later). Put some vodka, Sprite and any kind of red juice into a big bowl and throw in an ice ring. You'll have just classed up your college punch!

Just Say No to the Pre-assembled Platter

Whatever you do, *do not* buy these. For every veggie sliced and diced on a plastic plate, that's an extra $.50 out of your pocket. Grab a bag of chopped up broccoli and carrots at the grocery store, alternate colors and throw a sour cream dip in the middle. *Presto!*

Use Online Invites

You'll save on stamps and stationery by sending out EVITES (www.evite.com). They're fast and free and you can keep tabs on your guests from work when you're sneaking personal computer time.

Photos

Get your friend in art school to take black and white photos of the party. This'll make you look cool and artsy. If you want live music, contact a local music school in your area and hire a student or two to play. They'll love the exposure and won't charge you much.

Still nervous about throwing a party solo? Down a few of your own Jello shots before your guests arrive and let the festivities begin! You deserve this night!

Solo Travel

To take going out alone a step further, the concept of traveling solo is getting more exciting by the day. Pick a passion: cooking, hiking, mountain biking or hang gliding and you'll have your pick of companies catering to the solo traveler—more specifically, the solo female traveler. Here are some resources to get you started:

JourneyWoman – Offers a wealth of information for any woman traveling alone (or in a group) such as trip suggestions, safety measures and advice from solo women travelers around the globe. www.journeywoman.com

Savvytraveler.com – Another great website from the folks who bring you NPR's "Savvy Traveler" radio show, featuring a *Deal of the Week* section. www.Savvytraveler.com

REI Adventures – Offers a wide range of adventure trips for women. Not cheap by any means, but if you can splurge a little, you'll be in good hands. Log on to www.rei.com/adventures and click on the Women's Trips section.

Contiki Vacations – Caters to 18-35 years olds and lists specials for last minute travelers. Last time I checked, you could go to Spain and Portugal for $850 for two weeks. Now *that's* a bargain! www.contiki.com

Alpenhutte Lodge – Located in Colorado, the Alpenhutte offers affordable lodge packages catering to the solo traveler. Choose from dorm style or private rooms. www.alpenhutte.com

Mount Tremblant – You can get a fab spa package and your own condo at this Canadian mountain retreat located two hours north of Montreal, especially if you go off-season in the summer. www.clubtremblant.com

Web Fares – Spend five minutes logging on to a few airlines' websites and sign up for their last minute fares and packages. Every week you'll get a list of the last minute weekend specials with fares around $150. One note, you may have to fly back on a Monday to get the deal, so plan your trip accordingly.

Site59 – This is a fantastic resource for last minute vacation specials. Choose from a variety of flight, hotel and car packages around the world at affordable prices. www.site59.com

Priceline – You've wanted to try it but you're too scared, right? Well, it's good! If you're afraid to book the flight because you don't want to wind up changing planes five times, at least try it for the car rental or hotel. You can choose the level of accommodations you want in the city of your choice (sorry, you can't pick the hotel by name) and put in a suggested amount. Be careful. Once you commit to a price, your credit card will be charged. Be realistic too—you only get a few chances for the computer to accept your bid. For more information, log on to www.priceline.com.

But trust me here. This is a fantastic way to save money and score on five star accommodations!

Surviving the Holidays Solo

But alas, all vacations can't be surf and sun, ski lodges and hot cocoa. Yes, you will one day have to return home and deal with your relatives and their barrage of questions. And so, *goin' solo* gal, here are suggestions as to how to respond to Aunt Edna and the likes while sitting around your Thanksgiving table.

If your family says . . .	Your response is . . .
Why aren't you seeing anyone?	I'm too busy sleeping around to date anybody seriously.
Did you get a job yet?	No, but I've been asked back to two interviews at Hooters.
How long do you think you'll be able to pull this off?	As long as the President keeps extending unemployment, I think I'll be in great shape!

You think it's safe to live alone?	I paid off the drunk on my stoop so he makes sure no one follows me.
You know, (insert neighbor's name)'s daughter took a great job here. I'm sure she could introduce you to some nice people.	Nah. (They'll be waiting for you to say something else but you won't—really throws 'em for a loop.)
When do you think you'll move back home?	Once they clear my police record, I should be good to go.
It's just so hard out there. Why don't you come back home and live with us?	Only if I can turn the guest bedroom back into my bedroom and put pin-ups of Jon Bon Jovi on the walls. (They'll reneg on the offer immediately since they just painted.)
What happens if you get hurt?	I'll be fine, really. My neighbor plays a nurse on ER.
You must be lonely up there with no friends.	Who could be lonely with TIVO?
You know, I could call my friend Sylvia's cousin who has a nice nephew who works near you. He's very smart.	That's okay, thanks so much. It's actually a really small town and I met Matthew (make up name) already. We went out for drinks and wound up drunk in his apartment. I'd really feel awkward if Sylvia found out about it. You know how those things are, right, Grandma?

Some More Realistic Options

If eggnog and Christmas music make you want to hole up because you're just not where you thought you'd be at this time in your life, here are some additional (and more practical) suggestions to make the season a little more tolerable.

• **Pick one holiday party** – just one. Tell yourself it'll be the only one you'll go to during the season. Make a promise to yourself that you'll at least try to have a good time. Then, kindly decline the other invites (unless of course it's a work party you have to attend) and make other plans.

• **Stay away from the mall** – Right around October 31st, somebody somewhere decides it's time to start the Santa music. And while it's nice to hear for about a week, come December, you're just about ready to strangle somebody. The point of the matter is: Do your holiday shopping early so you don't have to get more depressed going to the mall, fighting off the crowds and hearing that blasted holiday music, which reminds you why you're depressed in the first place!

• **Volunteer** – One of the greatest ways to spend the holidays alone is to serve someone who's less fortunate than you. Not only will you feel good about yourself, you'll probably meet a few really nice people who may have similar thoughts as you about the holiday season. Call your local church, synagogue or community center to find out what holiday volunteer opportunities exist. In New York, try New York Cares (www.nycares.org). In Chicago, try Chicago Volunteer (www.chicagovolunteer.net). In Los Angeles, try Volunteers of America (www.voala.org).

• **Cook yourself a feast and rent a classic movie** – This is a favorite activity of mine on New Year's Eve. I cook something that I would never eat the rest of the year (Lamb, London Broil, some sort of white, flaky fish) and rent something in black and white. It's the ultimate escape and a lot of fun. Pick up a copy of *Solo Suppers: Simple Delicious Meals to Cook for Yourself*, by Joyce Esersky, Chronicle Books, for some tasty recipes.

• **Treat yourself to a massage or a facial** – Find out if there's an aesthetic training institute in your city and book yourself a facial! You'll pay next to nothing for a high quality treatment from a student-in-training. If you live in New York City, try the Aveda Institute in Soho 212.807.1492.

• **Get lost in a book** – Reading is a great way to lose track of time. Pick up a new memoir or get a recommendation from the librarian on a fun holiday read.

• **Clean** – Cleaning is a good way to let off steam. When you're done, you'll also have a great end result. If the holidays get you down, turn up the tunes and go to town with the Lysol.

• **Promises, Shmomises** – So you didn't quite lose that ten pounds you said you would last New Years. Big deal! Give yourself a break and pat yourself on the back for just being able to get out of bed and make it to work in the morning.

City Specific Solo Dates

The Equestrian

Boston

Boston Equestrian Center
44 McIntyre Rd., North Oxford, MA 01537
A short drive from Boston
508.987.6141
$45 / half hour

Chicago

Glen Grove Equestrian Center
9453 Harris Road (at Golf Road)
Morton Grove, IL
(15 miles outside of Chicago)
847.966.8032
$60 / half hour

Los Angeles

Los Angeles Equestrian Center
480 Riverside Dr. (in the Los Angeles Equestrian Center)
Burbank
818.569.3666
$60 / half hour

New York

Claremont Riding Academy
89th and Amsterdam Avenue
Upper West Side
212.724.5100
$60 / half hour (with instruction)

The Scavenger

Atlanta

Check out the Lakewood Antique Market located on the Lakewood Fairgrounds for an eclectic collection of antiques.

Boston

Spending a day in Essex will clear your head of all worries. While accessible via commuter rail, it's best to borrow a car for this thirty mile ride outside of the city. Take route 93N to 128N toward Gloucester. Get off at the first Essex Exit.

Chicago

Chicago Southland offers a row of antiquing in five historic communities: Blue Island, Beecher, Crete, Frankfort and Orland Park. You'll wind up spending the entire day in this quaint area. If you choose to stay inside the city limits, try the Chicago Antique Market at 47 West Division, open May-October on the last Sunday of each month.

Los Angeles

Get yourself to the Long Beach Outdoor Antiques and Collectibles Market at Veterans Stadium in Long Beach or the Santa Monica Airport Antiques and Collectibles Market.

New York

Take the Metro North train to Hudson, Tarrytown or Croton. You'll get lost in treasures. The fall is the best time of year to do this. Or, if you want to stay local, go to the Antique Market on 6th Avenue and 26th Street in Manhattan. It's only open on the weekends only so go early to see the best stuff!

San Francisco

San Francisco Design and Antique Mall will keep you very busy. It can be found at 701 Bayshore Blvd.

The Bounty Hunter

Atlanta

Tom Lowe Olympic Shooting Grounds
3025 Merk Road SW
404.346.8382
Trap and Skeet Shooting.

Chicago

West Chicago Gun Club
West Chicago, IL
630.231.9862
Trap and Skeet Shooting.

Los Angeles

LAX Firing Range
927 W. Manchester Blvd.
310.568.1515
Facilities include Indoor Pistol, Indoor Rifle and Shotgun Ranges.

Maryland

Gilbert Indoor Range
www.gilbertindoorrange.com
1022 Rockville Pike
Rockville
301.217.0055
You'll spend $145 to take a training course and get certified, but once you are, you'll pay only $29 per day to fire on their range.

Miami

Trail Glades Range Inc
17601 S.W 8th Street
305.226.1823
Outdoor Pistol, Outdoor Rifle, Trap and Skeet Shooting.

New York

West Side Pistol Range
20 West 20th Street
212.243.9448
$50 will get you a private lesson on firearm safety with an instructor, a .22 rifle and fifty rounds of ammo. Cool leather outfit sold separately.

San Francisco

Pacific Rod & Gun Club
520 John Muir Drive
415.586.8349
Indoor Rifle, Trap, Skeet, Sporting Clays and Archery.

The Food Connoisseur

Atlanta

Cooks Warehouse
www.cookswarehouse.com
549-I Amsterdam Ave. N.E.

404.815.4993

Among their numerous classes: the Spanish *Tapas* Party, The Rustic Italian Farmhouse Supper, or the Hot Tamales class, for $45 each.

Chicago

Cooking Academy of Chicago

www.cookingacad.com

2500 West Bradley Place

773.478.9840

Offers mini classes on topics such as sauces, soups and bread making for not a lot of cash.

Los Angeles

Bristol Farms

www.bristolfarms.com

915 E. 230th St.

Carson

310.233.4752

Demo classes on a variety of cuisines offered in the evenings range in price from $20-$30 per person.

Miami

Chef Allen's

www.chefallens.com

19088 N.E. 29th Ave

Aventura

305.935.2900

For $50 a person, Chef Allen offers classes such as Tropical, Latin and Caribbean Cooking, New World Cuisine and Exotic Cuisines of the Mediterranean.

New York

Grandma's Secrets

640 West 138th Street

212.862.8117

Learn how to make sensational pies such as banana cream, coconut or lemon meringue for less than $50 a class. Grandma will also come to your home and do parties or individual lessons.

Cooking By the Book

11 Worth Street

www.cookingbythebook.com

212.966.9799

For around $100 (a little more pricey), you can choose from a variety of courses ranging from seasonal cooking to wine and urban lifestyle dishes.

Cooking by Heart

www.cookingbyheart.com

203.629.1831

Offers guided tasting parties in New York City and Connecticut for around $35 per person. A great idea for a group!

San Francisco

City College of San Francisco

Fort Mason Art Campus

www.ccsf.edu

Laguna & Marina Blvd - Bldg B

415.561.1860

With topics like "Hors d'Oeuvres Party for Thirty in Three Hours," "Cooking Tour of New Orleans," "Tuscan Style Chicken Scaloppini & Tiramisu" and "Cuisines of Tropical Asia" all for under $50 each, who could go wrong?

Washington, D.C.

What's Cooking?

Email only: whatsckng@aol.com

1917 S. Street N.W.

Learn how to cook in a small group in a townhouse kitchen located near Dupont Circle. Fun classes such as "The Indian Kitchen," "Chinese New Year" and "Spicy, Smoky, Southwest Brunch" cost $45 per person.

The Shopper

Chicago

McShane's Exchange

815 West Armitage Avenue

773.525.0282

Get a deal on gently worn quality clothing and accessories.

Daisy Shop

67 East Oak Street, 6th Floor

312.943.8880

A fun Gold Coast shop that sells gently-worn couture clothing.

Fox's

2150 North Halsted Street

773.281.0700

Lincoln Park shop with designer clothes at great discounts. There are also Fox's in New York, Connecticut and Florida too.

Los Angeles

The L.A. Fashion District

www.fashiondistrict.org

110 East 9th Street, Ste. A-1175

213.488.1153

Located roughly between Main St. and Wall St., you'll find a lot of great stuff here.

Boutiques on Melrose Avenue between La Brea and Fairfax Avenues.

Lots of trendy stores line this street. Just walk around and browse.

California Market Center

www.californiamarketcenter.com

110 East 9th Street

800.225.6278

Offers seasonal shows and even has permanent vendors. Can be hit or miss but worth a shot on a rainy afternoon.

New York

Century 21

22 Cortlandt Street

(between Church and Broadway downtown)

212.227.9092

This place is a zoo. But it's got everything from shoes to sheets at amazing prices.

H&M

The big one is on 50th and Madison Avenue, but there are others around the city. Here you'll find Euro-style fashions dirt cheap. You can also find these in Baltimore, Chicago, Philadelphia, Washington, D.C. and Boston.

New York Sample Sales

Log onto www.nysale.com and sign up for a free e-mailed listing of weekly sales from well-known designers. Going to a sample sale is a real trip. You'll fall over half naked ladies trying on clothes and you may even get into a fight with someone who tries to steal your bargain. This is especially true at the Barneys New York Warehouse Sale. But it's all part of the game!

Fine & Klein

119 Orchard Street

212.674.6720

Your mouth'll water over these designer handbags. Though sold at a deep discount, you can still wind up spending a bundle. Fun to visit, as it's located in the Lower East Side. Stop at Katz's Deli afterwards for a fat corned beef sandwich, the other half of which, you'll fit in your phat handbag.

Loehmanns

www.loehmanns.com

7th Avenue between 16th and 17th Streets

212.352.0856

(and the original in Riverdale)

5740 Broadway

718.543.6420

Though many complain that it's "not as good as it used to be," you can still get a great deal here on basics for work, such as suits and coats, not to mention shoes and handbags.

And even if you don't live in NYC, there are **Loehmann's Plazas** all over the U.S.

Goin' Solo Party Recipes

Cocktail Foods

Baked Brie

You'll need: 1 Brie wheel, 1 package Pillsbury Crescent Rolls

Prep Time: 2 minutes to unroll and wrap, 15 minutes to bake

Directions: Unroll crescent rolls into a big square (don't break off at dotted lines) and lay Brie wheel inside. Wrap sides up around cheese and pull off extra pieces that are too long. Bake at 300 degrees for ten minutes or until top is brown and bubbly. Yummm. . . .

Spinach Dip

You'll need: 1 package frozen spinach, 1 package Knorr's Vegetable Soup Mix, 1 cup mayo, 1 cup sour cream
Prep time: 10 minutes
Directions: Thaw, rinse and dry spinach. Mix everything together. Chill for at least 2 hours before serving.

Pigs in Blankets

You'll need: 1 pack of hot dogs, Pillsbury Crescent Rolls (*if you make the baked Brie, you can use the remaining pieces from the crescent rolls)
Prep time: 15 minutes
Directions: Cut hot dogs into bite size pieces. Wrap bits of crescent rolls around the pieces leaving ends of hot dogs sticking out. Bake for 10-12 minutes at 350 degrees. Serve with mustard.

Stuffed 'Shrooms

You'll need: mushrooms, bread crumbs, chopped onion, garlic, celery and whatever other veggie you have in the drawer, olive oil, salt and pepper, Parmesan cheese
Prep time: 20 minutes
Directions: Wash and take the stems off the mushrooms. Put stems in a bowl. Chop onion, garlic and celery into tiny pieces (or mince if you have a blender) along with mushroom stems. Stuff this mixture into the mushroom caps and top with Parmesan cheese. Drizzle with olive oil and bake at 350 degrees until golden brown (about 15 minutes).

Hummus

You'll need: hummus
Prep time: none (1 minute if you put it in your own dish)
Directions: Just buy it pre-made and serve with pita bread.

Seven Layer Dip

You'll need: 1 package shredded cheddar cheese, 1 container prepackaged guacamole, 1 container sour cream, 1 can bean dip, 1 can sliced black olives, bag of tortilla chips

Prep time: 10 minutes

Directions: Layer everything one by one in a round dish, starting with the bean dip, guacamole, sour cream, cheese and olives. Serve with tortilla chips.

Ridiculously Easy Cheese Dip

You'll need: 1 block Velveeta cheese, 1 jar of salsa

Prep time: 5 minutes

Directions: This is so easy you'll laugh. Put the block of Velveeta into a bowl and dump in the salsa. Microwave for 2-3 minutes, or until cheese melts. Mix and serve. Your guests will be astounded at the flavor and think you spent hours on this recipe. If cheese dip gets cold, just stick it back in the microwave.

Hot Hors d'Oeuvres

You'll need: One word—COSTCO. Buy Wiltons Hors d'Oeuvres in the frozen food section. You can't go wrong with these things. You'll get a box of little spinach pies, puff pastries and mushroom thingies all in one box.

Prep time: 10-15 minutes (all baking time)

Directions: Open box. Throw everything on a cookie sheet and bake according to directions.

Brunch Ideas

Pasta Salad

You'll need: 1 box of shaped pasta, 1 jar of Italian dressing, cut up vegetables

Prep time: 15 minutes

Directions: Cook pasta according to directions. Toss with cut up veggies and Italian dressing. Chill until serving time.

Quiche

You'll need: Quiche

Prep time: 15-20 minutes (bake time)

Directions: Buy a frozen one and bake as directed. You see where I'm going, here?

Omelets

You'll need: eggs, scallions, shredded cheddar cheese, mushrooms, peppers, black beans, sour cream, salsa

Prep time: 20 minutes

Directions: Put each topping in a bowl on the table. Have your guests pick the combo they want and make an omelet. You remember how to cook eggs, right? If you can't do the omelet flip (I can't), just do a scramble. It tastes better anyway.

Desserts

Ice Cream Sundaes

You'll need: 2 gallons ice cream, whipped cream, sprinkles, cherries, hot fudge

Prep time: 5 minutes

Directions: Promote this as a "make your own sundae" event.

Hello Dollies

You'll need: 1 stick butter, 1 can condensed milk, 1 cup graham cracker crumbs, 1 cup chocolate chips, 1 cup shredded coconut.

Prep time: 8 minutes prep, 30 minutes bake time

Directions: Melt butter in bottom of 8"x 8" pan. Layer on top: crumbs, chocolate chips and coconut. Pour can of condensed milk on top and bake at 350 degrees for 30 minutes or until fork comes out clean. Cool and cut into squares.

Cookies with Kisses

You'll need: 1 package cookie dough (the ones sold in square chunks in the dairy section), ½ package Hershey Kisses, mini muffin tin

Prep time: 5 minutes (bake time 10 minutes)

Directions: Spray muffin tin with non-stick spray. Put 1 block of cookie dough in each hole and bake for 8 minutes. Remove from oven and place a Hershey Kiss in the middle of each cookie. Bake for an additional 2 minutes. Let cool for 5 minutes and serve warm.

Drinks

Sangria

You'll need: 1 bottle red wine, cut up oranges, apples, peaches, Sprite or 7-up

Prep time: 5 minutes

Directions: Pour wine into a pitcher. Add Sprite or 7-up

to wine to taste. Add cut up fruit and chill. This looks especially nice in a clear pitcher!

Champagne Punch

You'll need: 1 bottle Sprite or 7-up, 1 bottle cheap champagne, sorbet (any flavor), plastic Jello mold pan for ice ring, strawberries

Prep time: 10 minutes (make the ice ring the day before)

Directions: <u>For ice ring:</u> Wash and take stems off of strawberries. Fill Jello mold with water and drop in strawberries. Freeze overnight. <u>For champagne punch:</u> Combine champagne and Sprite or 7-up in a clear bowl. Add 5 or 6 scoops of sorbet and toss in ice ring as a finishing touch.

Some Closing Thoughts

It's a lot of information; I know. But there's so much more to write, so much more to research, so much more to explore. I barely feel as if I've skimmed the surface. I hope this book has given you a few of the tools you need to take the next step in whatever it is you're looking to do with your life. If you have suggestions for future editions of *Goin' Solo* (yes, they're already in the works!), I want to know. After all, your advice is what helps me the most. Please visit the website at www.goinsolo.net and click on *contact us* to send your suggestions.

Goin' Solo takes a lot of courage. But just because you're doing it alone doesn't mean you have to be lonely.

Useful Websites

Great general informational websites:

www.craigslist.org

Business, Starting Up

Business Marketing Supplies
      www.businesscards.com
      www.vistaprint.com
      www.modernpostcard.com

Business Incorporation
      www.mycorporation.com

Business Insurance
      www.netquote.com

Grants for Businesses
    – Foundation Center
        www.fdncenter.org
    – Small Business Administration
        www.sba.gov

Listing of State Tax Forms
      www.taxadmin.org
      www.irs.gov

Loans for Businesses
    – Office of Women's Business Ownership
        www.onlinewbc.gov

Online Payment for Websites
      www.paypal.com

Registering a Domain Name
      www.register.com

Small Business Assistance Center (SBAC)
      www.sbacnetwork.org

U.S. Trade Mark and Patent Office
      www.uspto.gov

U.S. Copyright Office
      www.copyright.gov

Women in Business Organizations
    – Assistance for women-owned businesses:
    www.onlinewbc.gov/docs/finance

- National Association of Women Business Owners
  www.nawbo.org
- Catalyst Women
  www.catalystwomen.org
- California/Los Angeles
  www.worksourcecalifornia.com
  www.lacity.org/cdd
- Chicago
  www.wehaveanswers.org
- New York
  http://www2.nypl.org/smallbiz/

Career Resources

Hollywood Digest
  www.hollywooddigest.com
Independent Filmmakers
  www.ifp.org
Women in Film
  www.wif.org
Women in New Media
  www.winm.org
Mediabistro
  www.mediabistro.com
National Concierge Association
  www.conciergeassoc.org
Doorperson / NYC Union
  www.sciu32bj.org
Women for Hire
  www.womenforhire.com
Women in Technology
  www.witi.com
Public Relations Society of America
  www.prsa.org
American Council on Exercise
  www.acefitness.org
Club Promoter Jobs
  www.joonbug.com
  www.impulsenyc.com (New York City)
Dog Walking
  - National Association of Professional Pet Sitters
  www.napdw.com

www.petsit.com

www.centrabarkchicago.com (Chicago)

www.centrabarkwest.com (New York City)

Teaching

www.kaplan.com

www.scoreprep.com

www.afterschoolmatters.com (Chicago)

Temping

www.staffingthecity.com (Chicago)

www.chicagojobs.org

Non-profit work

www.npo.net (Chicago)

Cell Phone Comparisons

www.getconnected.com

Cooking Classes

Atlanta

www.cookswarehouse.com

Chicago

www.cookingacad.com

Los Angeles

www.bristolfarms.com

Miami

www.chefallens.com

New York

www.cookingbythebook.com

www.cookingbyheart.com

San Francisco

www.ccsf.edu

Washington, D.C.

whatsckng@aol.com

Food Co-Ops

Atlanta

www.sevandana.com

Boston

www.harvestcoop.com

Chicago

www.coopmarkets.com

Los Angeles

www.coopportunity.com

New York
> www.4thstreetfoodcoop.org

San Francisco
> www.rainbowgrocery.coop

Gyms (Cheap)

Chicago
> www.lakeviewymca.org
>
> www.websterfitness.com

Los Angeles
> www.24hourfitness.com
>
> www.centerforyoga.com

New York
> www.lenoxhill.org
>
> www.dolphinfitnessclubs.com

Health Insurance

Quotes
> www.ehealthinsurance.com

Membership Organizations Offering Insurance
> – Writers Guild
>> www.wga.org
>
> – Screen Actors' Guild
>> www.sag.com
>
> – Authors' Guild
>> www.authorsguild.org
>
> – National Association of the Self-Employed
>> www.nase.org
>
> – New York City Freelancer's Union
>> www.workingtoday.org

Home Decor

> www.interfacflor.com
>
> www.surefit.com
>
> www.overstock.com
>
> www.ikea.com
>
> www.target.com
>
> www.walmart.com
>
> www.homedepot.com

Chicago
> www.afordableportables.net
>
> www.roomandboard.com

New York

> www.abchome.com
>
> www.gothiccabinetcraft.com

San Francisco

> www.sjfm.com

Washington, D.C.

> www.easternmarket.net

Housing

City information sites:

> www.homestore.com
>
> www.fodors.com
>
> www.findyourspot.com

Atlanta

> www.freeapartmentlocators.com
>
> www.homestore.com
>
> www.creativeloafing.com

Boston

> www.bostonapartment.net
>
> www.bostonapartments.com/alpha.htm
>
> www.resourcecapitalgroup.com
>
> www.roommateconnection.com

Chicago

> www.theaptconnection.com
>
> www.chireader.com
>
> www.apartmentpeople.com
>
> www.chicagoapartmentfinders.com
>
> www.icmproperties.com
>
> www.kassmanagement.com
>
> www.secondcityrentals.com

Los Angeles

> www.homestore.com
>
> www.apartments.com
>
> www.laweekly.com
>
> www.recycler.com
>
> www.aptmag.com
>
> www.roommatematchers.com
>
> www.roommateaccess.com

Miami

> www.rentmiami.com

New York City

> www.nofeerentals.com

www.nofeeapartments.net
www.ardorny.com
www.manhattan-skyline.com
www.keyah.com
www.betinaequities.com
www.villagevoice.com
www.roommatefinders.com
San Francisco
www.therentalsource.com
www.fordrealestate.com
www.litkeproperties.com
www.saxerealestate.com
www.apm7.com
www.renttech.com
Seattle
www.seattleapartmentfinder.com
Washington, D.C.
www.rentnet.com
www.smithapartments.com
Information on Renter's Rights
   – General
     www.rentlaw.com
   – New York
     www.tenant.net
   – California
     www.dca.ca.gov/legal/landlordbook
   – Renter's Insurance
     www.apartments.com

Leisure

Board Games
   www.areyougame.com
Car Rental
   www.rentawreck.com
Party Invitations
   www.evite.com

Mental Health

Cognitive Therapy
   – Academy of Cognitive Therapy
     www.academyofct.org

- Beck Institute
  www.beckinsititue.org
- Association for Advancement of Behavior Therapy
  www.aabt.org
- American Institute for Cognitive Therapy
  www.cognitivetherapynyc.com (New York)

Psychoanalysis
- New York Freudian Society
  www.nyfreudian.org

Psychiatry
- American Psychiatric Association
  www.psych.org

Psychology
- American Psychological Association
  www.apa.org

Social Work
- National Association of Social Workers
  www.socialworkers.org

Holistic Therapy
- National Institute of Health
  www.nlm.nih.gov/medlineplus/
  alternativemedicine.html

Art Therapy
www.arttherapy.org

Music Therapy
www.musictherapy.org

Anxiety Disorders Association of America
www.adaa.org

Low-Cost Therapy Centers
- Chicago
  Access Community Health Network of
  Chicago
    www.accesscommunityhealth.net
- Los Angeles
  The Los Angeles Free Clinic
    www.lafreeclinic.org
- New York
  Center for Educational and Psychological
  Services
    www.tc.edu/ceps
  National Institute for the Psychotherapies

(NIP)
>www.nipinst.org
– San Francisco
Therapy Network
>www.therapynetwork.net

Money Management

Money management / budgeting
>www.bankrate.com/brm/calc/Worksheet.asp
Budget-Minded Banks
– National Chains
>www.washingtonmutual.com
>www.wachovia.com
– Boston
>www.easternbank.com
>www.sovereignbank.com
– Chicago
>www.midamericabank.com
>www.northcommunitybank.com
– Los Angeles
>www.wellsfargo.com
– New York
>www.amalgamatedbank.com
>www.icbny.com
Credit Card comparisons
>www.bankrate.com
Debt and Money Consultation (fee-based service)
>www.myvesta.org
Investment Resources
>www.financialmuse.com
>www.morningstar.com
>www.learningannex.com
Mortgages
– Calculation
>www.bankrate.com
– Research
>www.lendingtree.com
Student Loans
– Student Loan Consolidation
>www.studentaid.ed.gov
>www.loanconsolidation.ed.gov

www.finaid.org
– Central Database of all Federal Student Loans
www.nslds.ed.gov

Taxes

www.irs.gov

Shopping, Discount Clothing

www.hm.com
www.loehmanns.com
Los Angeles
– L.A. Fashion District
www.fashiondistrict.org
– California Market Center
www.californiamarketcenter.com
New York
– Sample Sale Information
www.nysale.com

Travel, Solo

Journey Woman
www.journeywoman.com
Savvy Traveler
www.savvytraveler.com
REI
www.rei.com/adventures
Contiki Vacations
www.contiki.com
Alpenhutte Lodge
www.alpenhutte.com
Spa at Mount Tremblant
www.clubtremblant.com
Last Minute Travel
www.site59.com
www.priceline.com

Volunteering

New York
www.nycares.org
Chicago
www.chicagovolunteer.net
Los Angeles
www.voala.org

About the Author

Adina Kalish Neufeld has been living on the cheap in places she can't afford for over ten years. Foolishly determined to make life tolerable in the most expensive city in the nation, she moved to New York in 1993 to pursue her passion of writing and has been happily surviving ever since. She has since written for *The New York Times, Glamour, Mademoiselle,* ABC Television, as well as for numerous websites and corporate clients. In between writing gigs, Adina travels to colleges and universities around the country presenting her post-college survival seminar, *The Way It Is*. She has never paid a fee for an apartment, has held more internships than she cares to admit, spends entire weekends perusing Target and enjoys taking herself out on dates on a regular basis. From working as a toy dog at trade shows to building her own wall to convert a one-bedroom apartment into two, she doles out only tried and true advice that she herself has lived by while starting out in the big city.

If you'd like to ask her questions, go to her website: www.goinsolo.net.

Index